W9-BWK-875

John Green

Studies in Young Adult Literature
Series Editor: Patty Campbell

Studies in Young Adult Literature is intended to continue the body of critical writing established in Twayne's Young Adult Authors series and to expand it beyond single-author studies to explorations of genres, multicultural writing, and controversial issues in young adult (YA) reading. Many of the contributing authors of the series are among the leading scholars and critics of adolescent literature, and some are YA novelists themselves.

The series is shaped by its editor, Patty Campbell, who is a renowned authority in the field, with a forty-year background as critic, lecturer, librarian, and teacher of YA literature. Patty Campbell was the 2001 winner of the ALAN Award, given by the Assembly on Literature for Adolescents of the National Council of Teachers of English for distinguished contribution to YA literature. In 1989 she was the winner of the American Library Association's Grolier Award for distinguished service to young adults and reading.

John Green

Teen Whisperer

Kathleen Deakin
Laura A. Brown
James Blasingame Jr.

ROWMAN & LITTLEFIELD
Lanham • Boulder • New York • London

Published by Rowman & Littlefield
A wholly owned subsidiary of The Rowman & Littlefield Publishing Group, Inc.
4501 Forbes Boulevard, Suite 200, Lanham, Maryland 20706
www.rowman.com

Unit A, Whitacre Mews, 26-34 Stannary Street, London SE11 4AB

British Library Cataloguing in Publication Information Available

Library of Congress Cataloging-in-Publication Data

Deakin, Kathleen.
John Green : teen whisperer / Kathleen Deakin, Laura A. Brown, and James Blasingame Jr.
p. cm. — (Studies in young adult literature ; no. 49)
Includes bibliographical references and index.
ISBN 978-1-4422-4996-7 (cloth : alk. paper) — ISBN 978-1-4422-4997-4 (ebook)
1. Green, John, 1977- 2. Authors, American—21st century—Biography. 3. Young adult fiction—Authorship. I. Brown, Laura A., 1971- II. Blasingame, James. III. Title.
PS3607.R432928Z58 2015
813'.6—dc23
[B]
2014049731

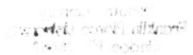
Printed in the United States of America

For Andrew and Madelyn: laugh, learn, and love; and for Michael who taught me how to do all three.

For my parents, to whom I owe everything, and for Steve, who brought music and wonder back into my life. I am forever filled with love, joy, and gratitude.

To Margaret Blasingame (1928–1986), who believed that all children are special and all children can learn.

Contents

Chapter One

The Road that Circled Back

Becoming John Green

The majority of successful young adult authors have certain things in common, including a week-to-week routine that consists of writing, conferencing with editors, rewriting, book launching, promoting, touring, winning awards, taking short breaks to renew their creative genius, and starting the process again. Although John Green fits this profile, there is something more to him, an additional dimension and a personal style that is hard to capture in a bottle: predictable but surprising; stable yet enigmatic; aloof but deeply caring; hip but homespun; Hollywood but also Indianapolis; and irreverent but deeply spiritual. Robert Frost tells us the road we take in life can make "all the difference," and perhaps it is the unusual road Green has taken that explains how he has become one of the most widely read and beloved authors of his time, a road that often circles back to where he began.

Green was born in Indianapolis and would return there as an adult to raise his own family, after living in a number of other places in Michigan, Alabama, and Illinois. But how did this son of a Nature Conservancy administrator and a community organizer become one of the most well-known and admired people in the world? The story is one that keeps coming back to the same two things, a desire to help others and a love for writing.

THE EARLY YEARS

Green's passion for writing engaging stories about the human experience did not begin with *Looking for Alaska* but surfaced during his childhood in Orlando, Florida. Green explains in his video blog (vlog) *Before* Looking for Alaska how he wrote and constructed a book, entitled *The Best New Year's Resolution Ever Happy New Year Streamers*, complete with color illustrations on every page.[1] The book, written when he was "a child," depicts the events of one New Year's Day three years earlier, when John's mother required every member of the Green family to make a New Year's resolution. Green reads the story to a subscribed Vlogbrothers audience of 2,306,139—256,479 of whom have viewed this video. His tone is tongue in cheek, but the hyperbole and underlying themes of the story show parallels with the novels he has written as an adult.

As Green reads the pages of the book and displays them on the vlog, he stops at times to comment on the meaning of symbols in the story, including a stairway in the Green home. John, the child, stands at the top, while his brother and parents stand on the ground floor. The stairway doesn't appear to go anywhere, and as Green explains, by his child logic it represented wealth. "The definition of rich was that you had stairs in your house." He believed that the IRS would charge each household's annual taxes on a scale based on the number of stairs in the house, a belief that may not be so far from wrong given that property value assessments are related to square feet and square feet do have a relationship to the number of stairs in a house.

The Best New Year's Resolution Ever Happy New Year Streamers tells the story of each family member's resolution and the likelihood of it ever happening. John's mother vows to clean out all the drawers, something she apparently had not done in many years. John's father promises to "weigh under six hundred pounds," which younger brother Hank points out is the same resolution as he made the year before and which John says "would be a miracle." Hank, who resides at the bottom of the stairs of wealth, resolves to take a bath, which older brother John says has never happened before. The resolutions in the story appear to be hyperbole, or products of a child's imagination. Nevertheless, they do provide archetypes: a mother who never quite gets all the housework done, a father who is fat (and perhaps inactive), and a younger brother who is stinky and unappealing. As in most autobiographical children's books, Green himself is the hero, the only one who actually succeeds in achieving his resolution, "to try my hardest."[2] Here in this first Green literary creation we have a cast of characters, all of whom are aspiring to take charge of their lives, and one admirable character who leads them all by succeeding in accomplishing what others only aspire to. Is this the Green formula for plot building? Perhaps so! Green's family life as a child was nurturing and emotionally healthy, and he often expresses gratitude for the love and support his family has given him throughout his life. Upon receiving the 2006 Michael L. Printz Award for Excellence in Young Adult Literaturefor his very first novel, Green acknowledged the qualities he most appreciates about his family:

> I would also like to thank my parents and my brother, Hank. I had the astonishing good fortune of having my parents by my side when the Printz committee called to tell me about this award. I have an extraordinarily kind and funny and supportive family—in terms of their goodness, they are possibly even better than librarians—and I'm so glad to have my mom and dad here tonight. My greatest ambition in life is to make them proud.[3]

Despite having the love and support of a "tight-knit family," however, Green characterizes his early teen years as filled with "a lot of existential despair."[4] "As a teenager, I found life as it is sort of unacceptable and paralyzing."[5] He also remembers being "very awkward socially without a lot of friends."[6] Green elaborates about his experiences at Glenridge Middle School and Lake Highland Prep, explaining that he was bullied, albeit by kids who had emotional problems of their own. One of his few friends, Matthew Brown, explained, "He was bullied by the tough kids at Glenridge, and then by the rich kids at Lake Highland. . . . John was always kind of eccentric: He was into Bob Dylan when the rest of us were listening to Milli Vanilli."[7] Another close friend, Andrew Sutherland, described Green as "a smart, sensitive kid labeled a nerd by some bullies."[8]

Instead of burying these experiences deep in his psyche, Green uses them for material in his realistic fiction: "I had the social disconnection to be a writer. . . . You need to be an observer. I think that stuff started in Orlando."[9] He responded on Vlogbrothers to a Tumblr message from someone who had attended the same Orlando middle school as he did, Glenridge Middle School, and even had one of the same seventh-grade teachers. He said that Green had been "a quiet, unique, and miserable boy . . . and was bullied because of [his] awesomeness."[10] Green remembered fantasizing about revenge at the time, "making them feel as scared and powerless as I felt," but he "realizes now that the people who bullied me were not evil. They were just kids living with their own fear and pain, some of whom were dealing with trauma and abuse that I never even could have imagined." This insight enables Green to understand now that their treatment of him had nothing to do with his value as a human being; it wasn't about him at all.

He remembers that it "was very difficult to feel anything but miserable in those days; in retrospect I survived middle school because many people were quite kind to me: my parents, teachers, fellow nerds, and even popular strangers who wouldn't stand for bullying."[11] He goes on to explain that he would eventually come to the conclusion that society as a whole decides what is acceptable behavior, and it is generally good and kind actions. He credits this as the premise at the heart of the Nerdfighters' international effort to make the world a better place. He goes on to quote John Darnielle, lead singer and songwriter for the popular indie rock band the Mountain Goats, when the band appeared at Carnegie Hall: "This is a message to sixteen-year-old me. Not only did you survive, but you are playing piano at Carnegie Hall."

Green continues in the vlog, explaining that very few miserable teens will ever be superstars performing at Carnegie Hall, but the point is that it is "ridiculous" to think that the teen years must be the best of your life. He ends the video with a quote from Robert Frost: "The only way out is through."[12]

HIGH SCHOOL SHENANIGANS

Nevertheless, life continued to have this sort of misery until Green enrolled at Indian Springs, a boarding school outside of Birmingham, Alabama, where he made good friends and became "kind of the court jester."[13] "When I was younger, I just wanted everyone to like me," Green remembers.[14] He enjoyed his new life at Indian Springs and especially playing the class clown.

The Indian Springs experience would become fodder for his first novel, a book that includes a tragic event—the death of a classmate—but also some "court jestering." That autobiographical ingredient in *Looking for Alaska* was the boarding school senior prank. Green's protagonist, Miles Halter, attends Culver Creek Preparatory High School, a boarding school outside of Birmingham, Alabama, nearly identical to

Green's alma mater. In real life, Green's family members became legendary for the scope of their senior prank, including Green's uncle, who traversed the dormitory circle clad in nothing but the American flag.

Green's own senior prank included a pretend prank to "lull the school administration into a false sense of security."[15] Close to midnight, Green and his buddies ignited nearly $300 worth of fireworks on campus, including several M-80s, now illegal, but then the largest legal explosive available for entertainment purposes. Green describes this as "an ocean of fireworks, underneath the dean of students' bedroom, and underneath the head master's bedroom."[16] The school administrators sprang into action, albeit barely dressed, and apprehended Green and his cohorts, all of whom were sentenced to manual labor on the school grounds for eight hours every Saturday and Sunday and four hours every weekday. This was not, as Green points out, the actual senior prank but just a setup to get the school administrators off their guard.

The actual senior prank perpetrated on the Indian Springs School community was the graduation speaker, supposedly selected by the senior class, but actually arranged by Green and his coconspirators. They allegedly contracted a famous professor of adolescent psychology to give a talk, but when the speaker launched into a lecture on "Adolescent Sexuality and Identification after Puberty," bawdy music began and the "professor" turned out to be an exotic dancer, who disrobed on the stage in front of "650 people," including parents, faculty, and all six grades of the school.[17] This is nearly identical to what happens in *Looking for Alaska*, except that the exotic dancer in the book is a man, while the real-life performer was female (and topless).

ALMOST A CHAPLAIN

It is not only charmingly affirming of his devotion to young people but also somewhat unexpected to discover that John Green began his adult career as a hospital chaplain working with kids.

In 2000, he had just graduated with a double major (English and religious studies) from Kenyon College, an Ohio liberal arts school highly renowned for its rigorous academics; in fact, seniors at Kenyon study far more hours than those at any other school in the nation.[18] In addition, to graduate from Kenyon, students must complete an exhaustive project, not unlike a master's thesis or a mini-dissertation. Classes are small and expectations are high. As Green would later explain, "Writers also have to read a lot, and my high school and college teachers taught me to love reading, which has been vitally important to me. Also, my education gave me some foundation for knowing how to write—both in the 'how to tell a story' sense and in the 'how to use a semicolon' sense."[19]

Green graduated from Kenyon and headed for an Episcopal seminary, intent on becoming a minister. His training included an internship as a hospital chaplain whose role was to counsel the families of terminally ill children.[20]

Green's lifelong spirituality is undeniable. In a blog post from September 23, 2008, he says, "I don't talk about it very often, but I'm a religious person. In fact, before I became a writer, I wanted to be a minister. There is a certain branch of Christianity that has so effectively hijacked the word 'Christian' that I feel uncomfortable sometimes using it to describe myself. But I am a Christian."[21]

At the heart of his code of ethics is the Golden Rule, which he explains: "First, there is the question of loving thy neighbor as yourself, which Jesus states clearly and irrevocably is the second most important law for his followers, behind only the love of God."[22]

Green's self-identification as a Christian surfaced with the young adult (YA) crowd, even before the vlogs and interviews in which he talks about his original vocation of Episcopalian minister. In an April 3, 2007, website posting, Green refers to *Looking for Alaska* as Christian fiction. Even Green himself admits that the content of the novel would not lead anyone to suspect that at its heart, *Alaska* is actually a story "about the kind of forgiveness that happens even though it is not possible."[23] Green goes on to explain that he does not believe writing can ever be amoral, no matter what the writer's intention may be. Green describes himself as feeling "somewhat uncomfortable with the notion that fiction teaches lessons. But I think it does." He also thinks fiction should teach us lessons: "I'm trying to preach in my books—because A. all my favorite books teach and preach without doing so professedly, and B. writing can't be apolitical anyway."[24]

In an interview for the blog *Seven Impossible Things before Breakfast*, Green explained that four hundred hours of serving as a student chaplain was required for his ordination and by serving real people at the hospital he was hoping to move from an intellectual experience to one steeped in "the reality of joy and suffering."[25] During this interview in 2007, he explained why he dropped out: "I loved the work, and

I doubt I'll ever do anything that important again. But it really tore me apart. I so admire the chaplains and social workers in hospitals, but I couldn't bear it. I didn't have the kind of faith that could encounter the truth of suffering without breaking, I guess."[26] Green talked at great length about his chaplaincy experience when he gave the Printz Award acceptance speech in 2006. After attending seminary classes during the day, Green would "sit alone in this little windowless room with these two beepers all night long. I would try to read or sleep, but mostly I just stared at the beepers and prayed they wouldn't go off. And then they'd go off."[27] Green reflects on how the beeper always took him to some "horrifically sad event," after which he would return to his isolation where he would think about "loss and guilt, and forgiveness," themes that would eventually show up in his books.[28]

THE WRITER EMERGES

Recognizing simultaneously both the importance of the work and his own emotional limitations for performing it, Green chose another path and aspired to be a writer. After his tour of duty as hospital chaplain, Green moved to Chicago, where he worked for *Booklist* as a publishing assistant and book reviewer. He was assigned to retype a lot of ISBNs and also to retype Printz Award speeches, by Walter Dean Myers, Laurie Halse Anderson, Ellen Wittlinger, and others. Reading these speeches introduced him to a genre he never knew existed.[29] Eventually, he was assigned to write reviews of YA books. "I was 22, and I think the people in the Books for Youth department thought, 'Hey, this guy is basically a YA himself, which led to them encouraging me to read (and eventually review) YA books."[30] He also did writing for *All Things Considered* on National Public Radio.

To Green himself, his apparent vault to the top of YA stardom probably seemed more like a slow, focused climb. He credits legendary *Booklist* editor and children's author Ilene Cooper with being a key mentor in the process, even providing her own editing services for the early *Alaska* manuscript. *Alaska* underwent two years of revision under Cooper's tutelage and two more years under another legendary editor, Julie Strauss-Gabel from Penguin. Green remembers that process: "Between when I sold the book and when it was published, about 80 percent of the words changed. It was a very long process, but quite fun."[31]

The success ratio of aspiring writers to successful writers is not very good, however, and Green is quite humble about his accomplishments and carefully reflective about his own behavior. In a 2004 monolog for *All Things Considered*, Green talked about the parallels between his own life and the life of the novel-writing uncle for whom he was named. Uncle John, John Thomas Goodrich, whose novel *Cotton Cavalier* was published in 1932, was twenty-seven at the time. Green, whose first book, *Looking for Alaska*, was about to come out at the time of the radio program, was also twenty-seven. John Goodrich was an alcoholic who moved to Hollywood with fantasies of the good life, which he envisioned as making millions on movie scripts and enjoying one big, never-ending, gin-soaked party. Green reveals that Goodrich instead lost his wife, his livelihood, and his dream of being a superstar writer. Green goes on to relate "two troubling facts" about the parallels he shared with his late uncle: "affection for booze, and a compulsion to move to Los Angeles." Green describes Goodrich's ailment as "'gettin' above your raisin'," when someone abandons the values of his or her upbringing, usually in exchange for a hedonistic lifestyle.

Finally, Green describes how he avoided making the same mistake his uncle had. Entertaining a fantasy of "going home every night to my Hollywood mansion and rolling around in a pile of $100 bills," Green was conflicted by the realization that "this is not a fantasy commensurate with the values of my raising." And then he found himself at a party, under the influence, and on the verge of succumbing to the same fantasy as his uncle had. *Looking for Alaska* was about to hit the shelves, and his second novel, *An Abundance of Katherines*, had just been accepted for publication. He was on a trajectory toward superstar success, but the seeds of his own destruction were also sown along the way should Green take that ill-advised path. Luckily for all of us, he recognized the disaster that lay down that road. He returned to his home in the Midwest, redoubled his efforts at writing young adult novels, married, had two children, and found new ways to minister to young people.

Green recognizes good fortune in the form of his beloved wife, Sarah Urist, who also attended Indian Springs School. In his Printz Award acceptance speech, Green expressed his feelings about Sarah.

There's one more collaborator who needs to be mentioned here, and that is my wife, Sarah. Sarah and I attended the same high school—a place that bears some physical resemblance to Culver Creek Prep—but we never knew one another until just after I began revising *Alaska* in earnest. So much of her, and so many of her stories, went into this book. *Alaska* says one thing in particular that I stole directly from Sarah: On our very first date, Sarah said, "Imagining the future is a kind of nostalgia." So I want to thank you, Sarah, for that line, for making each day of my life fun and invigorating, and for agreeing to marry such a nostalgic bastard.[32]

HOLLYWOOD SUPERSTAR

Eventually, of course, despite Green's premonitions about moving to Hollywood, Hollywood would come to him there at home in Indianapolis. In 2014, *The Fault in Our Stars* debuted as number 1 at the box office during its first weekend and grossed $286 million over the summer.[33] The movie starred teen heartthrobs Shailene Woodley and Ansel Elgort. The film adaptation of *Paper Towns*, starring Nat Wolff, Halston Stage, and Cara Delevingne, is scheduled to debut in June 2015.[34] *Looking for Alaska* was originally set for production but was shelved by Paramount, until the success of *The Fault in Our Stars* convinced them to reconsider.

By 2014, John Green had become a pop culture phenomenon, and like most pop culture icons, information defining his popularity is readily available on the Internet. In fact, FamousBirthdays.com reifies exactly how popular he is as "ranked on popularity based on boosts and other user activity" by the web editors:

- Number 1 most popular author from Indiana
- Number 2 most popular person born on August 24
- Number 5 most popular author of all time
- Number 7 most popular person named John
- Number 8 most popular person from Indiana
- Number 16 most popular person born in 1977
- Number 673 most popular person in the world

Competition is pretty stiff in these categories too. In the ranking of famous authors, for example, Green is surpassed only by William Shakespeare, J. K. Rowling, Anne Frank, and Dr. Seuss. He ranks ahead of such noteworthy writers as Stephen King, Roald Dahl, Mark

Twain, and Charles Dickens. This is not bad for Indianapolis's favorite son, who outranks even Larry Bird (French Lick) in pure Indiana popularity, although behind Michael Jackson.

In the end, John Green's essence and magic as a pop culture icon is found not only in his books but also in his daily life, of which he spends large portions sharing his ideas, values, and interpretations of the world with the public. On Vlogbrothers, he and his brother Hank provide strands of wisdom for life that hold millions of viewers attentive every week. Jessica Grose of *Mental Floss* may have summed it up best: "It's this hyper-contemporary combination of endless curiosity, Internet community engagement, and a do-gooder spirit that has made Green the pied piper of a certain kind of young nerd. Not only can he spin a great yarn, he's pinpointed the next generation's sweet spot, somewhere between self-reflection and the desire to do good."[35]

NOTES

1. John Green, *Before* Looking for Alaska (vlog), Vlogbrothers, YouTube, January 27, 2009, accessed September 1, 2014, https://www.youtube.com/.
2. Ibid.
3. John Green, "The Printz Speech," John Green, September 19, 2006, accessed September 8, 2014, http://johngreenbooks.com/.
4. Cynthia Leitich Smith, "Author Interview: John Green on *An Abundance of Katherines*," Cynsations, December 4, 2006, accessed September 3, 2014, http://cynthialeitichsmith.blogspot.com/.
5. Brian Farrey and Jonathan Stephens, "Author Interview," Teenreads, October 2006, accessed September 8, 2014, http://www.teenreads.com/authors/john-green/news/interview-100906.
6. Smith, "Author Interview."
7. Hal Boedeker, "John Green of 'Fault in Our Stars' Found Inspiration in Orlando," *Orlando Sentinel*, June 4, 2014, accessed November 2, 2014, http://articles.orlandosentinel.com/.
8. Ibid.
9. Ibid.
10. John Green, "On School Misery," Vlogbrothers, YouTube, November 19, 2013, accessed November 2, 2014, http://www.youtube.com/.
11. Ibid.
12. Ibid.
13. Smith, "Author Interview."
14. Farrey and Stephens, "Author Interview."
15. John Green, "John Green's Legendary High School Prank," Ransriggs, YouTube, December 8, 2007, accessed September 7, 2014, https://www.youtube.com/.
16. Ibid.
17. Ibid.
18. Daniel De Vise, "Five Colleges Where Students Study," *Washington Post*, May 22, 2012, accessed September 1, 2014, http://www.washingtonpost.com/.
19. Farrey and Stephens, "Author Interview."

20. Marc McEvoy, "Interview: John Green," *Sydney Morning Herald*, January 21, 2012, accessed September 1, 2014, http://www.smh.com.au/.

21. John Green, "Faith and Science," John Green, September 23, 2008, accessed September 1, 2014, http://johngreenbooks.com/.

22. Ibid.

23. John Green, "Christian Fiction," John Green, April 3, 2007, accessed September 1, 2014, http://johngreenbooks.com/.

24. Ibid.

25. Julie Danielson and Eisha Prather, "Seven Impossible Interviews before Breakfast #19: John Green—Printz Winner, Nerd Fighter, WorldSuck Decreaser," *Seven Impossible Things before Breakfast: Why Stop at Six?* (blog), April 13, 2007, accessed September 1, 2014, http://blaine.org/.

26. Ibid.

27. Green, "The Printz Speech."

28. Ibid.

29. Ibid.

30. Colleen Mondor, "John Green and the Power of YA Books," Chasing Ray, October 2, 2006, accessed September 8, 2014, http://www.chasingray.com/.

31. Smith, "Author Interview."

32. Green, "The Printz Speech."

33. "The Fault in Our Stars," Box Office Mojo, 2014, accessed September 1, 2014, http://www.boxofficemojo.com/.

34. "*Paper Towns*," Internet Movie Database, 2014, accessed November 2, 2014, http://www.imdb.com/.

35. Jessica Grose, "The Green Movement," *Mental Floss*, January 15, 2014, accessed October 28, 2014, http://mentalfloss.com/.

Chapter Two

The Pen *Is* Mightier . . .

After devoting much of his career to working as a publishing assistant and production editor for the *New York Times Book Review* and *Booklist*, John Green took the young adult literature world by storm in 2006 with his debut novel *Looking for Alaska*. This book introduced readers to *real* teenagers enrolled in a boarding school and searching for the "Great Perhaps." A recipient of the Michael L. Printz Award and the Teens' Top 10 Award, among other honors, this book introduced an author whose teenage characters attempt to assimilate themselves in a world full of addiction, death, identity, love, and loss. His second novel, *An Abundance of Katherines*, published in 2006, was also a Michael L. Printz Honor book. *Paper Towns*, published in 2008, was the recipient of the 2009 Edgar Award for Best Young Adult Mystery. His book *Will Grayson, Will Grayson*, published in 2010 and coauthored with David Levithan, appeared on the *New York Times* children's best-seller list. And his latest novel, *The Fault in Our Stars*, published in 2012, remained on the *New York Times* best-seller list for several months after its release. Green's books have been translated into fifteen languages and are best sellers worldwide.

These novels reveal characters who navigate through their circumstances and echo to some of the great voices in literature. Often wiser than their adult counterparts, and certainly smarter than their peers, these protagonists remember the words of Walt Whitman, T. S. Eliot, and William Shakespeare, to name a few. Readers—especially teenage readers—must *believe* in the characters they read about in order to identify with them; they must engage in the adventures and mishaps of characters, settings, and stories. Green presents witty protagonists who aren't heroic or beautiful in the conventional sense but rather ordinary and flawed. They are *human* and they are *real*.

GREEN'S ACCESSIBILITY TO HIS READERS

Perhaps the most unique aspect of John Green as a writer for young adults is his accessibility. His website is updated daily, and he communicates with his fans through Twitter, which also broadcasts a live feed on his website. On January 1, 2007, Green and his brother embarked on 365 days of text-less communication, Brotherhood 2.0. These daily conversational videos, uploaded and available on YouTube, chronicle a yearlong correspondence between Green and his brother, Hank, and their commentary about self, society, and relationships. Readers frequently remark that they have viewed the series in its entirety more than once. In a world where technology often evolves quicker than many can keep up—certainly quicker than the school system can—it is refreshing to have an author who is not only accessible but also stripped down to a webcam close up. Viewers are given a realistic, albeit magnified, view of Green while engaging in his everyday antics. And while this endeavor has ended, the spirit of it led to another forum for the followers of John and Hank: Nerdfighters.ning.com.

DFTBA inspires the mission statement of this ning. A common acronym among Green's followers, DFTBA (don't forget to be awesome) stands as an inspirational mission statement that fuels an Internet writing community ninety-three-thousand-plus members strong. Fellow nerdfighters enter a forum "where nerds gather and play" and "fight to increase awesome and decrease suck."[1] The site offers book recommendations, music suggestions, and nerdfighter projects (writing contests and such), but most importantly it provides an opportunity for readers to post their thoughts and videos about societal issues. There are rules and guidelines to the site that head off inappropriate content, and the site itself is a testimony to Green's deep respect for the adolescent voice. His novels don't patronize teens; they are sophisticated and profound, and this forum echoes that sentiment.

So, what is it about this voice in young adult literature that warrants and receives such a loyal following?

THE CONTRACT

A man who tells secrets or stories must think of who is hearing or reading, for a story has as many versions as it has readers. Everyone takes what he wants or can from it and thus changes it to his measure. Some pick out parts and reject the rest, some strain the story through their mesh of prejudice, some paint it with their own delight. A story must have some points of contact with the reader to make him feel at home in it. Only then can he accept wonders.

—John Steinbeck

This contract between readers and writers depends greatly on these "points of contact" that foster the relationship Green has with his readers, especially adolescents. His characters are honest but often lost in the unforgiving social world of youth. The injustices of the world frequently pose the greatest obstacles for these young protagonists, and their victories are celebrated after periods of great loss and much despair. Green's characters reflect the teenage search for power in a world that typically usurps and suppresses their effectiveness.

This contract, however, is not solely dependent upon the authors' ability—or lack of it—to connect with their readers. Rather, the contract is consensual. Green places a great deal of trust in his reader when he sets forth fictitious characters in fictitious settings facing real problems. Harold Vine and Mark Faust, in *Situating Readers: Students Making Meaning of Literature*, posit that "each member of the same social group experiencing a familiar cultural situation may share a common sense of its general nature, yet have a different sense of its particular meaning."[2] And thus, Green's readers have a common understanding of the general nature of their situation, and yet the meaning they take from it differs greatly: the situation is universal; the implications are not. Green echoes this notion of the contractual relationship and subsequent responsibility between writer and reader when he admits, "I think the writer's responsibility is to tell an honest story (which is also, I would argue, definitionally [*sic*] a hopeful story) and to make it as a gift to the reader. The reader violates the contract when s/he reads poorly or distractedly or ungenerously."[3] Arguably, the reader could not possibly read distractedly or ungenerously from any of Green's novels because they foster this consensual relationship from beginning to end. One only has to access Green's Twitter feed for evidence of this phenomenon.

THE SEARCH FOR IDENTITY

Chimpanzees, while they are very smart and interesting creatures, cannot tell each other stories about war heroes fighting sirens and a cyclops
to get home. They cannot use such stories to shape their values and their
relationships and their worldviews. We can, and do, and this engagement with constructed narrative is (imho) a big part of what makes us
human.

—John Green

One of the transcendent characteristics of young adult literature is its
ability to capture the adolescent's search for identity. Identity is often
revealed through the protagonist's exposure to and struggle with situating himself or herself in social and moral situations. Theorists like
Lawrence Kohlberg and Erik Erikson have provided a solid foundation
that helps foster an appreciation for the psychological changes that
occur during these adolescent developmental stages.

Lawrence Kohlberg chronicled the stages of moral development
that articulate how consciences form, operate, and change one's opera-
tions as one matures.[4] As an individual progresses through life, the
conscience progresses as well. Moral choices are based on external
forces like fear of punishment, personal gain, social influences, maintaining order, social contracts, and individual desire for and understanding of justice. The Levels of Moral Development are further di-
vided into three stages: the Preconventional, Conventional, and Post-
conventional/Autonomous, or Principled Level. Adolescents are typically situated in between the Conventional and Postconventional levels
because they are grappling with conformity and independence.[5] The
protagonists in Green's novels have developed beyond the Conventional level. That is, they are no longer loyal to the conformity that was so
comfortable to them earlier in life. Rather, these teens are seeking
autonomy; they pursue definitions of their own values and question the
validity of authority. It is important to note that these stages emphasize
moral thinking rather than moral behavior, so readers are therefore
privy to the moral struggles of these edgy teenagers through Green's
depiction of their thought processes.

Erik Erikson, a psychoanalyst, studied the psychosocial development of the ego and demonstrated how youth use conflict for creative
and constructive purposes. He posited that individuals need to orient
themselves into the "social" world, and doing so during stage 5 (occur-
ring roughly from ages twelve to eighteen) thrusts the adolescent into a

struggle between identity and role confusion. Ego identity represents the more positive aspect of adolescence, where the adolescent is establishing his or her "self," whereas role confusion occurs when the development of self appears contradictory with the role one must play.[6] Green's characters embody both ends of this spectrum of development: *Looking for Alaska*'s Miles Halter, in search of meaning, abandons his normal life to become part of a boarding school culture; *Paper Towns*' Colin Singleton, an official "dumpee," embarks on a journey to define his own relationship with relationships; *An Abundance of Katherines*' Quentin Jacobsen, a seventeen-year-old misfit, journeys to discover what is real and what is not; and *The Fault in Our Stars*' Hazel Lancaster grapples with the injustice of mortality. Green's protagonists develop a multitude of new ways to look at and think about their worlds. Parents in Green's novels aren't absent by any means, just distant. His teenage protagonists, therefore, are often situating themselves apart from their authority figures, not out of rebellion, but out of a quest for autonomy. This new interpersonal dimension, according to Erikson,[7] poses several challenges that once overcome will help teens to arrive at a sense of psychosocial identity. They gain a sense of who they are, where they have been, and where they are going, and they transition from home, both literally and figuratively, to the outside world.

The teenage protagonist, then, represents more than a character on the page. He or she represents the journey toward identity, a search for sense of self. And if the adolescent is embarking on a similar journey, Green's characters provide insight with which the adolescent reader can identify. Moreover, the identity novel serves a much greater purpose. James Blasingame, in *Books that Don't Bore 'Em*, suggests, "If the emotional and psychological urges of adolescence are such powerful forces, then harnessing them for the purposes of reading and writing instruction, as well as meeting the developmental needs of students, seems much more logical than attempting to swim against the tide."[8] Educators can use these novels to engage the young adult reader. And given the notion that readers vicariously experience the novels they read—the contract between the writer and reader—"then the benefits of reading widely in helping them resolve the issue of identity should be obvious."[9]

AUTHENTICITY

This is not so much an author's note as an author's reminder of what
was printed in small type a few pages ago: this book is a work of fiction.
I made it up.

   Neither novels nor their readers benefit from attempts to divine
whether any facts hide inside a story. Such efforts attack the very idea
that made-up stories can matter, which is sort of the foundational as-
sumption of our species.

   I appreciate your cooperation in this matter.

   —Author's note, *The Fault in Our Stars*

It is evident that there is a disconnect between the literature taught in
middle and high school classrooms and the literature teens are actually
reading outside the classroom. Green's books are read because, while
fictitious, they are authentic representations of the adolescent voice and
struggle. While steeped in real situations, the characters, setting, and
situations are fictitious. His books are authentic in their authenticity.

   When asked about the difference between fiction and lying, Green
aligns his writing with William Faulkner's premise that fiction is more
interested in truth than fact. Fiction, according to Green, reveals truth
through its deliberate attempt to ignore fact. His characters embark on
their moral, psychosocial journeys in fictitious places, which reveals
their truth. His motivation for their stories, however, is born from many
of his own experiences: "My particular high school experience pushed
me toward writing about 1. the South, and 2. smart kids, and 3. teenagers removed from direct parental control, and I also probably—4.—
owe this whole numbered-list-inside-a-sentence construction to high
school."[10]

   In fact, these rich experiences shape many of the settings in his
novels. The notion of paper towns, in his second novel, was born from
his experiences on a road trip across South Dakota during college.
Miles's boarding school, in his first novel, was shaped after the boarding school Green attended in Florida growing up. His narrative style
mirrors his own advice to teens about his own frequent practice of
reading and writing: "And the third thing, which I think is absolutely
vital, is to tell stories and listen closely to the stories you're being
told."[11] These stories become the premise for authentic literature. Nowhere is this more evident than in his latest novel, *The Fault in Our
Stars*.

Hazel Lancaster, while fictitious, embodies the spirit of a young girl named Esther, a nerdfighter who passed away from cancer in August 2010. Green admits, in an interview posted on his website, that "so much of the story was inspired by her and my friendship." Esther's story, however, is not Hazel's story. In fact, when Esther died, the premise of *The Fault in Our Stars* was vastly different: Hazel had not been created yet, and Green admits, "It was a vastly different story." What evolved, however, was a moving story about a fictitious teenager's experience with friendship, romance, and mortality: "Hazel is a fictional character, and she is in many important ways very different from the person Esther was."[12] Thus, the authenticity is what solidifies Green's contract with his reader; it seeks truth rather than fact. And the adolescent reader, caught in the chaos of seeking truth, finds perspective and understanding in his books.

CONTROVERSY

My friend David Levithan once said of gay writers, "We are political novelists who do not wish to be political." I feel a bit of that when it comes to banning books from classrooms and libraries. I don't want to have to fight that fight, but I won't shirk the responsibility I feel to my books and my readers.[13]
—John Green

It is no secret that adolescents are forced to deal with difficult issues both inside and outside of school. The world is a complex and unforgiving place, and adolescents are stuck between authority and autonomy. Young adult literature is a venue that speaks to them and for them.

The authentic problems and conflicts that authors like Green portray often invite controversy because of their depiction of the real and often raw struggles adolescents face. Green's protagonists do engage in risky behaviors: they smoke, they drink, and they engage in sexual relations. However, the depictions of the behaviors are not frivolous; rather, they help construct the psychosocial and moral development of the protagonists, which is not far removed from that of the adolescent reader. Green's first novel, *Looking for Alaska*, addresses relationships and intimacy. The characters connect through conversations fueled by alcohol and cigarettes. His most recent novel, *The Fault in Our Stars*, uses cigarettes as a power metaphor. Augustus Waters is never without one, yet he doesn't smoke. The cigarette cliché represents his power over a cancer causer. Many would argue the logistics of whether one book glorifies the practice while the other doesn't, but Green feels different- ly: "I think *Alaska* is more of an anti-smoking novel than *TFiOS* is (Hazel has that one little rant about cigarettes, whereas huge chunks of *Alaska* are devoted to exploring all the sad ways that smoking is a way of us expressing our desire to self-immolate)."[14] Controversial young adult content opens avenues for discussion and engagement.

In 2003, Michael Cart argued that young adult literature continues to increase in popularity among adolescents, and yet it remains contro- versial material in school.[15] In these novels adolescent protagonists often engage in experimental risky behavior. Some critics speculate that these stories might perpetuate questionable behavior. Blasingame, in a column about the banning of a young adult novel in a local school district, says, "We are preparing these young people for an adult world. Books provide a safe segue to places they will soon be going in per- son."[16] Controversial content in the young adult novel remains the crux of many legal battles between parents, school boards, and readers. But this literature allows the reader to see characters in their truest, albeit fictional, form. More importantly, through this literature students can expand their perspectives on the world.

TEXT AND MEANING

Steven Wolk, an associate professor of teacher education at Northeast- ern Illinois University, spent a year surveying students in local elemen- tary, middle, and high schools about what they were reading. Not sur- prisingly, several of the adolescents were only reading what was as- signed in school, most not even reading those books in their entirety. It was to this "assigned" reading that Wolk attributes the lack of desire to read outside of school. His study raises several questions for educators about what students are and should be reading, but most importantly he concludes, "Much of what students read in school should be interest- ing, provocative, critical, relevant, diverse, creative, emotional, and imaginative."[17] Few of the students surveyed used any of these charac- teristics to describe what they read in school. Green also feels that reader motivation helps to make meaning: "My intent as an author matters some, but you as the reader get some agency, too. You get to discover meaning within the story, and sometimes the meaning you discover will be meaning I hoped you would discover, and sometimes it will be meaning I could never have imagined you discovering. But together, we get to build something that matters."[18]

Thus educators should consider texts as a vehicle toward meaning, and if what we are providing to students is ineffective, why not consider something more relevant? English language arts teachers are asked to engage students in Key Ideas and Details, Author Craft and Structure, and the Knowledge and Ideas presented within a text (Common Core State Standards Initiative). Green has provided exemplary literary texts with which to do so.

NOTES

1. Nerdfighters, home page, accessed January 12, 2015, http://nerdfighters.ning.com/.

2. Harold A. Vine Jr. and Mark A. Faust, *Situating Readers: Students Making Meaning of Literature* (Urbana, IL: National Council of Teachers of English, 1993), 139.

3. John Green, interview with author, May 4, 2008.

4. Lawrence Kohlberg, *Essays on Moral Development*, vol. 1: *The Philosophy of Moral Development* (San Francisco: Harper & Row, 1981).

5. W. C. Crain, *Theories of Development* (New York: Prentice Hall, 1985).

6. Erik Erikson, *Childhood and Society* (New York: Norton, 1963).

7. Ibid.

8. James Blasingame, *Books that Don't Bore 'Em: Young Adult Books that Speak to This Generation* (New York: Scholastic, 2007), 6.

9. Ibid., 17.

10. John Green, *An Abundance of Katherines* (New York: Dutton, 2006), 252.

11. Ibid., 254.

12. John Green, "Questions About *The Fault in Our Stars*," John Green, 2010, accessed January 12, 2015, http://johngreenbooks.com/.

13. John Green, *Looking for Alaska*. New York: Speak, 2005.

14. Green, "Questions About *The Fault in Our Stars*."

15. Michael Cart, "Bold Books for Innovative Teaching: A Place of Energy, Activity, and Art," *English Journal* 93, no. 1 (2003): 115.

16. Valerie Strauss, "A Plea for Book Censors to Stand Down," *Washington Post*, September 23, 2013, accessed January 12, 2015, http://www.washingtonpost.com/.

17. Steven Wolk, "What Should Students Read?" *Phi Delta Kappan* 91, no. 7 (2010): 10.

18. Green, "Questions About *The Fault in Our Stars*."

Chapter Three

Navigating the Labyrinth

From the very beginning, I wrote this book for high school students.
—John Green

Miles Halter is an ordinary, self-proclaimed "regular shit" kind of kid who leaves his hometown in Florida in search of an interesting and eventful life. Suffice it to say that his past life was the opposite, and this new adventure promises what it lacked. Enrolling in Culver Creek boarding school brings new friends and new experiences that foster his discovery of what a person who is irreparably broken feels. But the novel is not without hope, as it invites teenagers to reflect upon their choices, their limits, and their identity. Young adult literature has been searching for an odyssey, a teenage epic like *Looking for Alaska*, since Holden left Pencey Preparatory in 1951.

Both J. D. Salinger and Green attended preparatory schools similar to that of their protagonists, and while the experiences of both teens are fictitious, they are *real*. Like Holden, Miles is not without flaws, but unlike Holden, Miles has a solid handle on his self-concept. He befriends a rebellious band of teenagers at Culver Creek, and together they encounter love, loss, and heartbreak. But this book does not tell your average teenage love story. *Looking for Alaska* tells a genuine, albeit raw, story about a group of adolescents trying to navigate through some of the toughest years of their lives.

THE JOURNEY

So this guy . . . Francois Rebelais. He was this poet. And his last words
were "I go to seek a Great Perhaps." That's why I'm going. So I don't
have to wait until I die to start seeking a Great Perhaps.[1]

The novel begins with a rather disappointing—although anticipated by
Miles—farewell party. Attended "by two vastly, deeply uninteresting
people," this party presents the crux of Miles's boredom: a series of
experiences that had simply met his expectations without exceeding
them. Consequently, he chooses to leave his mundane, ordinary life
behind and enrolls in Culver Creek—a school his father and uncles had
attended—in search of his own Great Perhaps. What connects most
with the reader in this novel is the candid honesty with which Green
juxtaposes the awkwardness and wisdom of the adolescent. The teens
in this novel attempt to situate themselves within the social and academic scenery at the boarding school, and in doing so, they begin to
question their own morals and the injustice of others'.

THE BOARDERS

I thought of the Great Perhaps and the things that might happen and the
people I might meet and who my roommate might be. . . . I hated sports.
I hated sports, and I hated people who played them, and I hated people
who watched them, and I hated people who didn't hate people who
watched them or played them.[2]

Looking for Alaska is actually Miles's story, narrated by him and
shaped through his encounters with love, with life, and with loss. Miles
is *not* a dysfunctional, angry teenager who hates his parents. He is *not*
an attractive young man who draws females like moths to a flame. He
is *not* filled with disgust at the injustice of puberty. Rather, Miles is
refreshingly normal and deceptively smart. He memorizes famous people's last words and is fascinated with the indelible marks people leave
on the world.

This young protagonist embodies the quizzical nature of adolescents
and their uncanny ability to adapt to life's adversity. His story is told
through a series of awkward events and encounters, all of which are the
result of this young man trying to find his way in a foreign, albeit
exciting, new world. Bored with his mundane existence, Miles enrolls
in a boarding school many miles from what he understands, and the

reader is drawn to both his sense of adventure and his willingness to forge friendships in an unfamiliar social circle.

Chip (the Colonel) Martin

> I saw a short, muscular guy with a shock of brown hair. He was hauling a gigantic army-green duffel bag through the door of my room. He stood five feet and nothing, but was well-built, like a scale model of Adonis, and with him arrived the stink of stale cigarette smoke.[3]

When Miles first arrives at Culver Creek, he meets Chip, or the self-named Colonel. The two boys are roommates, and Green is quick to distinguish between the two: Miles is skinny whereas Chip is muscular, Miles is unsure whereas Chip is confident, and Miles is clearly out of place whereas Chip is comfortable at Culver Creek. Consequently, it is Chip who welcomes Miles into the fold of new people and ultimately his "first badass moment."[4]

Chip, a student from New Hope, Alabama, is the antithesis of a young man attending a prominent boarding school: he is a smoker and a drinker; he is in a committed, dysfunctional relationship; he has been ejected from thirty-seven consecutive Culver Creek basketball games; and he despises wealth and privilege. The latter quality is a direct consequence of his own less-than-affluent upbringing. He is quick to position Miles at Culver Creek. He bestows the ironic nickname "Pudge" on Miles and introduces him to the catastrophic force that is Alaska. In essence, Chip is gregarious and easy to like.

Takumi Hikohito

> The sickest emcee in Alabama.[5]

Miles meets Takumi in the lunchroom where they bond over a "bufriedo." Quiet and rather subdued, he doesn't smoke like the others but still follows them to the Smoking Hole. Early in the novel, it becomes obvious that Takumi is the thinker of the group. He figures things out and is consequently the keeper of secrets. His character, while not as prominent as the others in the novel, adds a bit of grounding to the group. He is often the voice of reason and serves as comic relief. When invited into the planning of the preprank, he quips, "I hope you didn't bring the Asian kid along thinking he's a computer genius. Because I am not."[6] And he is known for his ability to rap on command. His role in the group becomes important during The After when he is shut out by Chip and Miles, both of whom can't seem to come to terms with their own guilt. In the end Takumi must reconcile his own demons before he too leaves Culver Creek in search of his Great Perhaps.

Lara Buterskaya

> By happy coincidence, a cute sophomore named Lara ended up sitting on my lap. Lara'd been born in Russia or someplace, and she spoke with a slight accent.[7]

While Alaska is Miles's romantic pursuit, Lara is his first sexual encounter. Introduced to him by Alaska, she serves to help Miles define his own feelings of romance. Ever present in The Before, Lara fades to the background during The After. During a rather awkward encounter toward the end of the novel, however, the reader becomes aware of the genuine nature of her character. Miles realizes that while she cannot fill the void left by Alaska, she is worthy of friendship and respect.

Alaska Young

> The hottest girl in all of human history was standing before me in cutoff jeans and a peach tank top.[8]

The novel's namesake, Alaska Young, represents the point at which the journey begins and ends. All of the adolescents in this story are searching to understand this chain-smoking, self-destructive, self-deprecating young girl. She is an impulsive and chaotic mass of contradiction. Alaska has a library of unread books, an irrational fear of ghosts, and a staunch dislike for misogynistic commentary. She engages in a variety of risqué behaviors and has serious intimacy issues. And yet the reader cannot help but fall in love with this beautiful, although flawed, young character. Miles too is helpless against her; he is drawn to her impulsiveness. While she is the antithesis of Miles, Alaska empowers him to embrace spontaneity and live in the moment.

The Weekday Warriors

In direct opposition to the other characters in the novel, there are the predictable boarding school types otherwise known as the Weekday

Warriors. Led by a young man named Kevin, this group is comprised of the wealthy and prominent members of Culver Creek. They are aptly named because they travel home to their air-conditioned mansions on the weekends. This group of students are the arch-enemies of Miles and his friends.

THE ADULTS

Another feature that sets this novel apart from other young adult literature is the presence of supportive adult figures. While the adults appear generationally and philosophically distant, they are held in relatively high regard by the adolescent characters. The book opens with Miles's parents throwing a farewell party for him, all the while trying to understand why their son has made the radical decision to leave. Rather than berate his journey as "immature" or "ridiculous," they are supportive and encouraging. Likewise, Chip's mother represents all that parents sacrifice for their children. The tensions between the adolescents and their parents in this novel are not the result of parents who just don't get it; rather, they result from much deeper circumstances, many of which Green explains.

Perhaps the most significant and paradoxical adult in the novel is Old Man Hyde. Hyde is introduced as a frail, unyielding, crotchety old teacher, and yet he helps to navigate the troubled youth in the novel toward truth. Hyde teaches world religions, an intellectual course that inquires about "the search for meaning" and the interconnectedness of life. Miles is drawn to his teachings and often reconciles the events that unfold in the novel through Hyde's spiritual and philosophical lectures.

THE MESSAGE

I know I say this all the time, but I really believe it: Books belong to their readers. And if I were to speculate about something outside of the novel, my voice would inevitably be privileged over the voices of other readers, and I really don't want that.
—John Green[9]

There is no doubt that the characters drive this novel. Green spent a great deal of time writing and rewriting them to make them all true to their stories. What engages the reader, however, are the ambiguities left at the end of the novel; it is through those questions that the reader can make meaning. Green speaks repeatedly about the contract between reader and writer and how he feels that meaning should be made through this relationship. He empowers the adolescent reader through his presentation of ideas like intimacy and friendship but leaves more questions than answers while showing mastery in the art of storytelling.

Ambiguity

> I wrote the book because I wanted to explore whether it is possible to reconcile yourself to that ambiguity, to live with it and not let your anger and sadness over the lack of resolution take over your life. [10]

When a novel leaves a reader with more questions than answers, it can be disconcerting. In Green's case, however, it is a stroke of genius. Throughout the novel, the characters seek the answers to a number of questions. Some are answered, many are not. At the beginning of the novel, Alaska recites the words of Simón Bolívar as quoted by Gabriel Garcia Marquez: "How will I ever get out of this suffering?" This question becomes significant or symbolic because it fuels the journey of the characters, all of whom are trying to navigate their own suffering. This labyrinth has no map, and it is the navigation of suffering that reveals each character's truth. Miles suffers through his attraction to a girl he will never have; Alaska suffers through a past she can't reconcile with; Chip suffers through trying to understand the loss of his dear friend; and Takumi suffers through his guilt. The After does not resolve anything, and thus the reader is left wondering how these young characters will deal with their suffering. In essence, this is a novel about loss and grief, about who gets to grieve more, and about how we fill the void left by loss. More importantly, though, it is a novel that while it leaves the reader pondering these notions, also leaves the assurance that ambiguity is the natural order of things.

Intimacy and Friendship

One of the most compelling threads of the novel is the notion of intimacy. Green's characters engage in physically and emotionally intimate moments, many of which convey both the inquisitive nature of adolescents and the awkwardness of youth. When Miles first meets Alaska, he is drawn to her frankness about relationships. He observes her uninhibited affection toward her boyfriend Jake and secretly wishes he was the recipient of the gestures: "I wanted to hate Jake, of course, but as I watched them together, smiling and fumbling all over each other, I didn't hate him. I wanted to *be* him."[11] Miles's admission of his jealousy is honest and forthright. He is drawn to her and yet cognizant of his distance from her physical affections.

From the beginning, theirs is a relationship built on depth of emotion. As the novel progresses, the reader is privy to Miles's thoughts about intimacy. He is always physically aware of his proximity to Alaska, and yet their encounters speak more to the emotions surrounding their relationship. Throughout The Before, Miles is confused about the amorous nature of Alaska: "irresistibly flirty one moment, resistibly obnoxious the next."[12] And it is this contradiction that establishes the most intimate moments in the novel. When the two are together just talking, their emotional bond is strong. However, when Miles seeks intimacy of a more physical nature, Green is quick to react with the uncertainty and awkwardness typical of such teenage encounters. Sex, in this novel, is not romantic and noteworthy at all. Rather, it is full of fumbling hands, uncomfortable movements, and little satisfaction.

One of the most controversial scenes in the novel occurs between Miles and Lara. Set to the backdrop of an old *Brady Bunch* rerun, Lara seeks to pleasure Miles, a kind of encounter neither has experienced before. As the show recounts the antics of the notoriously cheesy television family, Lara inquires about performing a sex act on Miles. The reader can feel the awkward tension between the two because neither can make a decision about what to do and how to do it. Green litters the passage with words like "weird," "nervous," and "quizzically."[13] All of this helps to further the confusing and embarrassing encounter. When both Miles and Lara are at a loss how to proceed, they seek Alaska's advice. What happens next is rather prosaic. Alaska demonstrates the act with a tube of toothpaste, a utilitarian product that couldn't be further removed from romance. Afterward, the tone shifts because both Miles and Lara are uncomfortable, so they go back to their homework. Both adolescents have engaged in a physically private encounter; however, it was devoid of any emotional engagement.

Later that night, Miles finally gets his opportunity to be physically intimate with Alaska. Again, this encounter is not presented with the romantic overtones worthy of such moments: "Our tongues dancing back and forth . . . she tasted like cigarettes and Mount Dew and wine and Chap Stick."[14] Miles treads cautiously, and Alaska concludes the encounter by calling it "fun."[15] What is especially salient about both of these encounters is not the idea of adolescents engaging in sexual situations but Miles's reactions after each one. Following his encounter with Lara, he reverts back to homework. Following his encounter with Alaska, however, he whispers words of love.

Throughout The Before, Alaska and Miles's relationship frequently involves highly emotional and private moments of sharing, of touching, and of just being together. And thus Green dichotomizes the notion of true love with that of physical gratification.

NOTES

1. John Green, *Looking for Alaska* (New York: Speak, 2005), 5.
2. Ibid., 8, 45.
3. Ibid., 9.
4. Ibid., 48.
5. Ibid., 43.
6. Ibid., 103.
7. Ibid., 51.
8. Ibid., 14.
9. John Green, "Questions About *Looking for Alaska*," John Green, accessed January 12, 2015, http://johngreenbooks.com/.
10. Ibid.
11. Green, *Looking for Alaska*, 72.
12. Ibid., 75.
13. Ibid., 127.
14. Ibid., 131.
15. Ibid.

Chapter Four

Will Grayson, Will Grayson

TWO HEADS ARE BETTER THAN ONE: TWO AUTHORS WRITE ABOUT TWO CHARACTERS WITH IDENTICAL NAMES

Opening at third place on the *New York Times* best-seller list among books for younger readers, *Will Grayson, Will Grayson* (*WG, WG*) was the first story with gay protagonists to show up in the newspaper's prestigious weekly rankings.[1] Talented and popular young adult author David Levithan cowrote *WG, WG* with John Green, alternating odd and even chapters. The authors passed the early chapters back and forth like a baton until the two eponymous Will Grayson characters met for the first time in chapter 7.

The premise of two characters with the same name originated with Levithan, who is often mistaken for a David *Leventhal* who, like Levithan, attended Brown University in the early 1990s, as reported by David Wiegand of the *San Francisco Chronicle*: "Now good friends, Levithan gave Leventhal an advance copy of 'Will Grayson,' including the partial dedication to him. That's when Leventhal told him that his college roommate was a kid named—wait for it—John Green."[2] Levithan's dedication reads, "To David Leventhal (for being so close)."

Green's dedication reads "To Tobias Huisman," in honor of one of the first patrons of Green's Nerdfighter's website discussion forums, who Green explains became "comfortable and open with his sexual orientation (he's gay) and also saw the many challenges that he faced with integrity and courage. He inspired a lot of the book, so I wanted to dedicate it to him."[3]

As the chapters rolled out, the two authors were happy to find themselves on the same page as they took a hard look at the issues of life. In an interview for US Penguin Group's website Books 4 Boys, Levithan explains that the two authors separately but simultaneously "decided to grapple with some very similar ideas. (Note: I don't say 'themes' here, because neither of us writes with 'themes' in mind.)"[4]

Green and Levithan's story is about two teenaged boys who revolve like moons around the planet. And the planet is their mutual friend the not-so-tiny Tiny Cooper, a gay high school football star. He is so large that Will Grayson marvels every day as "Tiny miraculously manages to wedge himself into the chair-desk beside mine in precalc."[5] Will, who is straight, and Tiny, who revels in being gay, have been best friends since childhood and have stood up for each other in numerous situations over the course of their lives. Will's chapters (odd numbers), told in first person, were all penned by Green. The other will grayson, always uncapitalized, meets Tiny purely by accident when their paths cross accidentally in downtown Chicago. Tiny, who "falls in love every hour on the hour with some poor new boy" according to Will, falls instantly in love with the other will grayson, who is also gay. The even-numbered chapters, told in first person by will, are the invention of Levithan. Although Will and will have antithetical home lives, they are both experiencing issues with identity resolution, involving self-image and peer relationships, that are leading them toward confusion and depression. Albeit from different perspectives, both protagonists are having a hard time figuring out how to navigate the intricacies of a relationship with a young woman who is a close friend but also loves them romantically.

Love of many varieties is at the center of this story. Will loves Tiny like a brother, and will loves Tiny as a boyfriend. Both Will and will find their relationships with Tiny at the center of their identity crisis. They both need to be loved, in different ways, but they must both love themselves before they can have a healthful relationship with another human being. Maura loves will like a boyfriend, but will loves Maura only as a friend. Jane loves Will like a boyfriend, and Will probably loves her back, but he may feel too much like damaged goods to engage with that love until he feels his brotherly love for Tiny reciprocated. And Tiny loves everyone, including himself, about which he is very demonstrative.

"THE PLAY'S THE THING"

Tiny's expression of his love for himself, his sexual identity, and for life in general manifests itself in a musical play, *Tiny Dancer, Hold Me Closer*, which he writes, casts, directs, and performs throughout the book. Not only is Tiny Cooper big, but also he has a big personality and lots of friends, enough friends to convince various school organizations to back the play. Both the high school's Gay-Straight Alliance and the student council vote to provide funding for Tiny's play, the mostly autobiographical story of Tiny's life told in song and dance. The casting, rehearsing, and revision of Tiny's play provide the backdrop for the real lives of its characters. The play is also a prime source of contention between Tiny and Will, although Tiny doesn't understand Will's feelings of betrayal and abandonment over the play.

From day 1, Will is convinced the play will result in his complete humiliation. He even asks Tiny to drop the whole thing, but Tiny thinks the play will have the opposite result and insists on naming a main character Gil Wrayson. Tiny wants Will to be in the play, but Will refuses; and Will wants the Will Grayson character to be written out of the play, but Tiny refuses. Jane opines that the play script looks great and Will should be flattered, but to no avail. Simultaneously, Tiny attempts what he perceives as a big favor to Will by playing the role of Cupid between Will and Jane, who has something of a crush on Will. Unfortunately, Will turns terribly awkward, confused, and flustered around Jane, always saying the wrong thing and regretting it later. To compensate, Will claims to Tiny that he doesn't care about Jane and to himself that he has mixed emotions about her, but he clearly cares for her.

In one particular moment of clumsiness, Will unintentionally insults Jane over a note she left for him in his jacket. A wrong choice of words turns serious flirting into serious rejection. When Will turns to Tiny for counsel, baring his soul to his friend as he usually does, Tiny fails to provide succor in his usual fashion. Will feels doubly rejected.

And so the cycle goes throughout the story. Tiny pushes Jane and Will together, Will can't cope, and Tiny is too busy with the play and his own love life to act as Will's emotional nursemaid, as he has done in the past. The play is too close to the truth for Will, and Tiny keeps on revising to get it closer to their real lives while claiming it is fictitious, thus pushing Will deeper into depression and frustration.

A BATTLE OF WILLS: CAN ONE WILL GRAYSON
REPLACE ANOTHER?

As the book approaches chapter 7, Will Grayson and will grayson are about to enter each other's lives on a cold winter evening in downtown Chicago. Prior to their rendezvous, they are both experiencing problems with a girl. In will's case it is Maura. All Maura claims to want is a straight answer (pun intended) to the question "Are you gay or straight?" Maura and Will are friends, but Maura wants more than friendship, and Will is offended that Maura feels entitled to assume he is gay just because he is not attracted to her. Their relationship is somewhat opposite to that of Tiny and Will, in which Tiny is theatrically open about his sexual identity but finds the idea of being romantic with his best buddy, Will, absurd if not disgusting. Unlike Maura, Will places the highest importance on his friendship with Tiny, even above a romantic relationship with Jane. Will really does love Jane, but until he gains enough confidence to put himself out there, he will continue to make excuses.

Will and will meet accidentally at Frenchy's, a porn shop in downtown Chicago. The latter believes this to be a first date with Isaac, with whom he thinks he has been talking online every day for months. When Isaac suggests they meet at a downtown establishment, will assumes it will turn out to be a trendy nightclub or coffee shop, not a tawdry sex shop. Sadly, there is no such person as Isaac, but only Maura, vindictively masquerading online and leading will on a wild-goose chase to a seedy location. Meanwhile, Will Grayson has been literally left out in the cold when his fake ID turns out to be flawed and he is refused admission to see the band Maybe Dead Cats at a nearby bar. Frenchy's may be an adult bookstore and sex shop, he reasons, but at least it will be warm inside.

During their chance encounter in the porn shop, the two Wills figure out that Isaac is a fraud, that will is gay, that Maura is a heartless fiend, and that the answer to all will's problems is just across the street in the rather large person of one Tiny Cooper. Tiny meets will; will meets this "ginormous guy" "with a broad smile" and "dimples the size of a baby's head"; Tiny heaps on the charm, and will is swept off his feet.[6]

Tiny's lifelong friend Will can be a frustrating contradiction to Tiny, for whom things seem so simple. Tiny brought Will and Jane together; Will acted disinterested; Jane went back her old boyfriend; and Will complained of rejection. Will brought will and Tiny together;

they like each other; and again Will feels rejected. In addition, the play continues into casting, and Will complains that he is relegated to second-class status: "I'm nothing but a bit character in the Tiny Cooper story, and there isn't a damn thing I can do about it,"[7] but there actually is something he can do in a passive-aggressive style, and that is to ignore his best friend at every turn. He refuses to share in Tiny's excitement over his new boyfriend, refuses to speak to him at all about anything.

But ignoring Tiny is like denying Mount Everest, and after Tiny expresses his emotional distress over being snubbed by his best friend, Will comes around somewhat. Tiny will rename the Gil Wrayson character Phil Wrayson, and Will insists that he should get to pick the actor who plays him. Will helps with auditions, and their friendship limps along.

Meanwhile, Tiny's romantic relationship with the other will grayson is rocky. Although Tiny is enamored of will and floored by the number of poetic texts he sends every day, their romance may be doomed from the start. As obsessed as Tiny is with living life to its fullest, will is equally obsessed with the negative aspects of his own life and life in general. If Tiny's proverbial glass is full to the brim, will's glass is shattered. When Tiny comes to dinner in the small apartment where will and his mother live, the experience is great for Tiny but painful for will: "I can't help it—I'm seeing our apartment through his eyes—our whole lives through his eyes—and it all looks so . . . shabby. the water stains on the ceiling and the dull-colored rug and the decades-old tv. the whole house smells like debt."[8] Tiny is not the least bit bothered and perhaps not aware that his own family's comparative wealth may be off-putting to his new beau. Tiny lives in a mansion and drives a Mercedes luxury car.

The problem is more than socioeconomic status, however; it has to do with self-concept, and will sees himself as a loser. When Tiny asks about will's father, will explains he doesn't know much about his father or even where he is, bringing on a panic attack in which will comes to the conclusion that he is just not capable of a relationship because of who he perceives himself to be.

Tiny is truly gallant, and will perceives that he is completely non-judgmental of will's family history, social status, or mental health. This is a new place for will but one he may not be comfortable with:

I am so used to bringing out the pain in people, but tiny refuses to play that game. while we're texting all day, and even here in person, he's always trying to get to the heart of it. and that means he always assumes there's a heart to get to. i think that's ridiculous and admire it at the same time. i want the something else he has to give me, even though i know it's never going to be something I can actually take to have as my own.[9]

Before will can love or be loved, he will need to love and accept himself. In a dramatic, unrehearsed ending to the play at the novel's end, that conflict may be resolved.

"ARE YOU FABULOUS?" CHARACTERS AND IDENTITY CRISIS

Will Grayson, Will Grayson is mostly about teens searching for and celebrating their identities, or as Patty Campbell, adolescent literature expert and longtime columnist for the *Horn Book*, once described the adolescent identity crisis, "Who am I, and what am I going to do about it?"[10] Most characters in the book seem to be doing one of the two: either trying to figure out who they are or shouting it out to the world.

Tiny Cooper, as we have seen, is an extremely large and lovable young man (over three hundred pounds), who plays high school football in Evanston, Illinois, and falls in love at the drop of a hat. He revels in his homosexuality even to the point of making jokes about himself and how many gay stereotypes he fits. Everyone loves Tiny; he has a heart to match his size.

Tiny has no problem with who he is, but he does have a problem with romantic relationships. He can never seem to get one to last or to be loved in return with the depth of feeling he has for others, and especially the significant other of the moment, whoever he may be.

Tiny is best friends with Will Grayson, and the two have been through a lot together over the years, taking turns standing up for each other. Tiny treasures their friendship more than Will realizes.

Will Grayson (capitalized) is a bundle of adolescent uncertainty, self-doubt, and clumsiness. He unsuccessfully attempts to avoid committing major faux pas by following "two very simple rules: 1. Don't care too much. 2. Shut up. Everything unfortunate that has ever happened to me has stemmed from failure to follow one of those rules."[11] Following these rules doesn't seem to work, however, and despite what he may pretend, he does care, deeply, and he cannot help but express his thoughts and feelings no matter how hard he tries to ignore them. Will has a very tender, easily injured heart. Will is figuring out that he is in love with Jane. Deep down he knows it, but in his adolescence-induced fog of hormones and emotions, he sometimes won't admit it.

He also knows that he loves Tiny as a brother, and that he is jealous when Tiny has a boyfriend or is in the midst of a big project, like the play. He will take the length of the book to sort all of this out, however. In contrast, will grayson (uncapitalized) is not only Tiny's important love interest in the book but also a sort of foil for Tiny's innocent naïveté. As joyous and rambunctious as Tiny is, will is equally pessimistic and introverted. His primary form of interaction with the world, when he is not working at CVS Drugstore, is online, a fact that makes him an easy target for Maura's cruel prank, the creation of a fictitious online persona, Isaac, who draws will into a love affair. Levithan explains that will writes his chapters in lowercase because

> that's how he sees himself. He is a lowercase person. He is used to communicating online, where people are encouraged to be lowercase people. His whole-self-image is what he projects in that space, and his one comfortable form of communication is when he's anonymous and sending instant messages. . . . It's how his self-expression has formed. Is it stunted in some way? Absolutely. [12]

He is breaking through some barriers, however, as the story rolls along. In a conversation with his mother about how things eventually have gone sour between him and Tiny, he asks her about her relationship with his father. Was it love? How did it turn "into hate and sadness"? His mother wisely explains, "Need is never a good basis for any relationship. It has to be more than that." [13] In the end, will may find a way to end his self-defeating behavior.

Jane Turner (in Evanston) is a sort of everygirl of sweetness and light, while Maura (in Naperville) is more given over to the dark side. Jane has strong romantic feelings for Will, whose behavior would easily turn any young woman away in anger. Nevertheless, she remains his friend and part of Tiny's circle even after apparent rejection. Maura, on the other hand, refuses to settle for friendship with will and seems only interested in what he can do for her as a boyfriend. When he fails to show romantic interest in her, she sets a trap for him online that can only break his heart (if it weren't for meeting Tiny Cooper that night at

Frenchy's). Jane may very well understand Will better than he understands himself, acting as a sort of gal-pal archetype throughout the
story, helping to manage the comatosely drunken Tiny, supporting
Tiny's play, and always being there for Will when he needs her and
when he finally comes to his senses and admits he's in love with her.

"THIS BAND IS SO COMPLETELY BRILLIANT!"

American indie rock bands and music are important to the story, especially Neutral Milk Hotel (NMH) and their album *In the Aeroplane
over the Sea*, which "sort of changed my life," according to Will. When
rumors of a reunion tour (the group broke up in 1998) have NMH
getting back together one night at the Hideout, a dive bar in downtown
Chicago, the plot pattern is set to accumulate the lead characters in the
same spot at the same time. In the real world, the band's lead singer,
Jeff Mangum, "became indie rock's resident recluse for over a
decade"[14] before the band really did reunite for a world tour that began
in 2013 and extended into 2014.[15] In *WG, WG*, however, the band that
actually performs at the Hideout, much to Will's disgust, turns out to be
fictitious Ashland Avenue, hoping to trade on Neutral Milk Hotel's
popularity by planting the rumor of a reunion.

The next time the characters head downtown, it is to see
Schrödinger and the Maybe Dead Cats, also a real band, who tweeted a
thanks and dedicated a performance to Green and Levithan on Twitter:
"Tonight's show is dedicated to @realjohngreen and David Levithan
who apparently wrote us into their new book, Will Grayson x2. Thanks
guys!"[16] In the story, Will's fake ID fails to gain him entry into the
venue because it gives his age as twenty instead of twenty-one, and so
Will heads for a nearby bookstore to kill time and there runs into his
namesake who has been sent there on a wild-goose chase by his friend
Maura. In the book, the conundrum of logic presented in the thought
experiment known as Schrödinger's cat becomes a metaphor for Will's
life. In 1935, Erwin Schrödinger invented a paradox to illustrate a
problem he saw in one of the concepts of quantum mechanics held at
the time. In this scenario, a cat was placed in a box with a flask of
poison that would be released when a source of radiation set off a
device that shatters the flask at some point in the future. In realistic
logic, the cat is either dead or alive and it is alive until it dies, but in
quantum mechanics reasoning at the time, because subatomic particles

were interpreted to be in more than one place at a time, the cat would be interpreted to be both dead and alive at the same time. This becomes the central metaphor for Will's life because he feels the confusions of holding opposing emotions at the same time. He loves Jane, but at the same time he does not love Jane, for example. These are the conflicting emotions common to adolescence.

NOTES

1. John Green and David Levithan, "A Conversation between John Green and David Levithan about Will Grayson, Will Grayson," US Penguin Group Books 4 Boys, November 2010, accessed December 10, 2013, http://www.us.penguingroup.com/.

2. David Wiegand, "Authors, Characters in Tandem in 'Will Grayson,'" *San Francisco Chronicle*, May 12, 2010, accessed December 19, 2013, http://www.sfgate.com/.

3. John Green, "WG, WG Questions Answered," Tumblr, Onlyifyoufinishedwgwg, January 12, 2013, accessed December 29, 2013, http://onlyifyoufinishedwgwg.tumblr.com/.

4. Green and Levithan, "Conversation."

5. Ibid.

6. John Green, *Will Grayson, Will Grayson* (New York: Dutton, 2010), 126.

7. Ibid., 112.

8. Ibid., 204.

9. Ibid., 215.

10. Roger Sutton, "An Interview with Patty Campbell," *Horn Book*, September/October 2010, accessed December 19, 2013, http://archive.hbook.com/.

11. Green, *Will Grayson*, 5.

12. Green and Levithan, "Conversation."

13. Green, *Will Grayson*, 249.

14. Evan Minsker and Amy Phillips, "Neutral Milk Hotel Reunite for Tour," Pitchfork, April 29, 2013, accessed December 29, 2013, http://pitchfork.com/.

15. Jenn Pelly, "Neutral Milk Hotel Expand Tour Again," Pitchfork, December 10, 2013, accessed December 29, 2013, http://pitchfork.com/.

16. Maybe Dead Cats, "The Maybe Dead Cats," Twitter, April 6, 2010, accessed December 29, 2013, https://twitter.com/MaybeDeadCats.

Chapter Five

An Abundance of Katherines

Colin Singleton has just been dumped by Katherine XIX. One might think it just a coincidence then that Colin has also been dumped by every Katherine he has ever dated, beginning with Katherine I, but Colin is certain there is more to it than mere chance. Colin, a seventeen-year-old child prodigy, speaks eleven foreign languages and is a master at anagramming even the most difficult words; relationships, however, continue to remain a mystery to him—but not for long. Colin is on a mission to find out why, in relationships, some people are always the "dumpees" and others the "dumpers." Thus, he creates a formula—the Theorem of Underlying Katherine Predictability—one he is certain will prove relationships can be mathematically determined. Heartbroken, and formula in hand, Colin heads out on a road trip with his one and only best friend Hassan to see if he can't uncover the "truth" about love. His journey leads him to the unlikeliest of places: Gutshot, Tennessee, and to Lindsey Lee Wells, the very first non-Katherine who just might drive Colin to rethink not only his formula but also his whole place in the world.

TELL ME A STORY

"Storytelling is the oldest form of education. People around the world have always told talks as a way of passing down their cultural beliefs, traditions, and history to future generations. Why? Stories are at the core of all that makes us human." [1]

In *An Abundance of Katherines*, John Green shows himself to be the ultimate storyteller. He takes us through the story of Colin Singleton, and through Colin's story he emphasizes the overall importance of stories in our lives. But in order to connect with adolescent readers, Green doesn't just "tell" the story; he effectively engages them in the story through clever, innovative means, making this more than just a simple young adult novel—it makes it a real adventure.

THE IMPORTANCE OF STORIES

More than anything, Colin Singleton wants to matter; he wants to be important in a way that is far greater than being a winner on the television show *KranialKidz*. Like many adolescents, Colin is trying to figure out his place in the world, to figure out who he really is, and this is one way Green captures his audience—by focusing on the universal truth that each of us, Colin included, is a product of our experiences, our stories. They help shape and define us, and through the sharing of these stories, we learn about each other and about ourselves. If readers can see themselves in Colin or in one of the other characters, they are more likely to want to keep reading.

To help readers develop an understanding of the importance of stories, Green ironically makes the protagonist Colin—a super brainiac—completely inept at storytelling. Even though Colin's experiences with nineteen different Katherines would seem to have all the makings for an incredible tale of love and loss, Colin doesn't understand how to put all of his experiences into a cohesive, meaningful narrative that others can understand. Colin instead sticks to math—something that is more reasonable and tangible—versus words to express his emotions. Lindsey tries to explain to Colin that a good story is more than facts and figures, to which Colin replies, "My theorem will tell the story. Each graph with a beginning and a middle and an end."[2] Colin is so concerned with finding his own truth, with proving his theorem correct, that he neglects to pay attention to the little things that have happened to him and continue to happen to him every day. Green, of course, shows us that it is the little things that actually make the story, not the big, obvious ones, and that truth is about what one chooses to see.

To further develop the importance of stories, Green centers part of the novel around Colin, Hassan, and Lindsey's involvement in the creation of "an oral history for Gutshot, for future generations."[3] In order to document life in Gutshot, Tennessee, the three characters interview residents about their memories of growing up and living in Gutshot. As they recall those stories that matter to them, the creation and development of the town (the setting) immediately comes to life for the characters and the readers. Colin and the others hear stories of everything from wanting to make sculptures with a chainsaw to shooting snakes—again, the little things, the things that don't necessarily seem important but matter. It is through these experiences and his conversations with Lindsey that Colin finally realizes his mathematical theorem cannot tell the whole story of love because there is so much more to tell than what a few plots on a graph can say.

As more and more characters' stories intertwine, Colin begins to develop as a storyteller. After telling Lindsey about the author Norman Mailer, Lindsey says to Colin, "That's a good story. See? You can tell a story."[4] This development continues as Colin and Lindsey share more of their experiences. At one point, Lindsey references the way one looks at stars as similar to the way one tells stories. In essence, we look for patterns. When we look at the night sky, we look for how the stars connect, which is how we see the constellations out of what seems to be a "big fugging random mess." Colin, she exclaims, thinks in this same manner; he is, therefore, "a natural born storyteller."[5] Soon after that, Colin finally does tell his own story—the whole thing—all the Katherines from beginning to middle to end, with morals and romance and everything a story needs to be real and true. And in the telling of his story, Colin realizes that even if he matters, the future will forget him at some point, but the stories will remain: "And he found himself thinking that maybe stories don't just make us matter to each other—maybe they're also the only way to the infinite mattering he'd been after so long. . . . Almost without knowing it, he'd started writing. The graphs in his notebook had been replaced by words."[6] While Green's story also comes to a quick close after this event, his words remain.

ELEMENTS OF A REALLY GOOD STORY

Since Green puts so much emphasis within the novel's story line on the importance of good storytelling, it is only right that he should work just as hard to keep readers wanting to read his novel by incorporating a number of interesting writing elements and techniques. One such technique Green utilizes most effectively is the blending of genres. While

An Abundance of Katherines may, on the surface, look like a traditional young adult novel, it is in fact quite nontraditional. The novel is a mix of elements from multiple genres within the same text. It creates a unique read and allows readers to see how multiple, sometimes seemingly dissonant ideas and elements can work together seamlessly to create one single story.

Footnotes are a common feature of nonfiction or informational texts. With a focus on vocabulary and extended details, this element is generally found in formal academic papers or educational textbooks and is designed to provide the reader with additional information to help with comprehension. In the case of *An Abundance of Katherines*, the purpose is much the same, but readers get more than just a few tidbits of information; they get a window into Colin's mind. Most of the footnotes serve to extend the depth of his character and the plot as a whole. With a third-person narrator, readers often lose that sense of intimacy with a character, as there is no "I" with which to make a personal connection. With the use of footnotes, however, Green makes up for that.

It is clear from the very beginning of the novel that Colin is incredibly smart and, often, socially awkward. However, the footnotes allow readers to more fully explore these character traits. At one point, Colin is lamenting his lack of employment skills, and this is emphasized through the inclusion of a fictitious want ad, in part that reads, *"Job duties include reading, remembering encyclopedias, novels, and poetry; and memorizing the first ninety-nine digits of pi.*[33]"[7] This last section of the ad, which does not necessarily seem to contain an important bit of information, includes a footnote, indicating to the reader there is more to know about this seemingly random fact. Upon reading this particular footnote, the reader learns that Colin memorized pi when he was only ten years old and then proceeded to create a sentence "in which the first letter of each word corresponded to the digit of pi (a+1, b+2, etc.; j=0)."[8] But Green doesn't stop there. He then includes the actual sentence Colin wrote when he was ten, starting off by stating, "The sentence, if you're curious:" By that point, how can we not be? Green keeps us strung along, entertained at every turn. Because it is mentioned that Colin knows eleven languages, Green also uses the footnotes to translate pieces of text: "Je m'allelle Pierre," Colin blurted out after the boys had introduced themselves. "Quand je vais dans metro, je fais aussi de la musique de prouts.[23]" The translation in the footnote reads, "My name is Pierre. When I go to the metro, I also make fart music."[9] Readers can see Colin's sense of humor in addition to his intelligence play out in the text. Each new footnote builds Colin's character, making him more and more real.

In addition to character development, the footnotes are also used to provide random details and historical facts woven into the novel's story line. Sometimes they are just simple statements that add a bit of detail. "Now, Colin had seen enough movies to know what happens when dorks go to cool-kid parties; generally, the dorks either get thrown into the pool[59] or they become drunk, vacuous cool kids themselves."[10] It seems an odd place to have a footnote, after simply mentioning being thrown into a pool; after all, there is nothing new or incredibly intriguing about being thrown into a pool and certainly nothing in the sentence that readers would have a hard time comprehending. But that's the fun in it; that's what makes the reader want to look to see what more could be said about such a mundane thing. In this case, the footnote reads, "Although there are admittedly not a lot of pools in Chicago." From this, the reader gains a small piece of information about the setting: Colin lives in Chicago. Is it necessary? No. Yet providing such small details gives the story a different level of credibility; it makes it all the more real.

Some of the historical facts woven into the novel include details regarding the Black Dahlia murder case. A successful California doctor by the name of George Hodel was, in all likelihood, the serial killer linked to this case. These details are seemingly thrown into the text during a discussion of Colin's IQ. The corresponding footnote, then, provides details into this man and into the specific statement that marks him as a serial killer. Because this information is included in the novel—a piece of fiction—it leaves the reader to wonder: is this really true, or did Green just make it up to fit in with the novel? That is all part of the fun. The reader wants to believe the narrator but is unsure. Just as Colin is searching for the truth, readers are as well. (I can tell you that the above information is true because I Googled it, which I am guessing is exactly what Green would want his readers to do.) To create a text that will make readers simply need to know more is ingenious. Reading thus becomes more of an adventure, as there is something new to discover on almost every page. And while these "asides" could be considered a bit distracting, they are, above all, new knowledge that can be applied to the story for a more enriching experience. There is no doubt adolescent readers will come away with a new appreciation for the way things are interconnected.

Green incorporates some other nontraditional elements in the novel that help further develop the story, including graphs and an appendix. Because the Theorem of Underlying Katherine Predictability is so important to the story, the reader finds graphs placed throughout the book as Colin plots each Katherine. These graphs, much like those you would find in a math textbook, help the reader visualize Colin's progression in his journey to find the "truth" about love, which is what drives Colin's story from the start. He wants to prove he can develop this theorem and that it works, and these graphs make the theorem tangible for both Colin and the readers.

The appendix, however, is where the real work on the theorem takes place. It is in the appendix that the reader discovers the theorem is real; it was actually developed by mathematician Daniel Biss. Over the course of ten pages, Biss takes the reader through the entire process of developing the theorem and plotting the points (Katherines) to show Colin's "Eureka moment."[11] Biss also mentions that while he does not believe in the theorem itself, there have been research studies conducted in which people have looked into the possibility of finding ways to use math to predict the staying power of a marriage. Once again, the reader is given the option: do I want to know more about this or not? Either way, the information is there for the taking.

Throughout the novel, Green is constantly forcing such questions on readers. He has an uncanny ability to anticipate what readers will want to know more about. While the footnotes, as previously discussed, are designed to answer some of these questions on the spot, the story itself takes a different approach; it too answers questions but only after the reader has had time to ponder a bit. For example, beginning on page 8 and continuing throughout the entire novel, Colin and Hassan both use the word "fug" or "fugger," which to me was clearly a substitute for the word "fuck." It was a noticeable substitution that made me wonder: why? After noting its consistent use, I as an educator wrongly assumed that the publishers must have put pressure on Green to remove profanity to ensure the book's success in schools and libraries. And then there it was, the answer revealed through the story itself, as Lindsey asks Colin, "Why the fuck do you and Hassan say fug all the time?" Colin explains it is because of Norman Mailer's novel *The Naked and the Dead*. Apparently, in the book, Mailer's editor changed every "fuck" to "fug," so they use the word "fug" "to pay homage to Mailer."[12] (And yes, I did look up this as well, and there it was: the words "fug" and "fugging" both used on page 10 of *The Naked and the Dead*). It is as though Green knew I would want to know about it, but he made me wait until one hundred pages in before he would reveal the truth. That's what will keep adolescents—and all readers—captivated by this story. Green utilizes a number of other techniques that give dimension and strength to his story. Flashback is one. These sections of the text, labeled "The End (of the Beginning)," "The Beginning (of the End)," and "The Beginning (of the Middle)" take us back and forth through Colin's memory, giving the reader additional insight into why Colin thinks the way he does and why he makes the decisions he does when it comes to love and relationships.[13] "Katherine XIX wasn't quite yet the XIX when they hung out alone together for the third time. Although the signs seemed positive, he couldn't bring himself to ask her if she wanted to date him, and he certainly couldn't just lean in and kiss her. Colin frequently faltered when it came to the step of actual kissing."[14] Most of these flashbacks occur after conversations Colin has with another character, when he begins to make connections between past events and new experiences in his life. The flashbacks, all in fragments, just like our own memories, are ultimately pieced together to create one whole story—Colin's story of the Katherines I–XIX.

Green also makes use of the mundane, which gives the story strong relatability with readers. So often novels avoid such trivial things as eating or going to the bathroom, but Green includes them all. Both Hassan and Colin eat breakfast, lunch, and dinner, go to the bathroom, take showers, throw up, sit and read, drive into town, and make phone calls. And it's during these everyday practices that things actually happen: conversations occur, decisions are made, and meaning is discovered, just like in "real" life: "Listen, *sitzpinkler*,[3] I'd love to comfort you, but I could put out a house fire with the contents of my bladder right now." Hassan breezed past the bed and opened the door to the bathroom. "God, Singleton, what'd you eat? It smells like—AHHH! PUKE! PUKE! AIIIIEEE!"[15] Once again, Green emphasizes the "little things" in life that are nonetheless important. These apparent minor details keep the reader involved and are integral to Colin's struggle to know that he matters.

Green also creates an effective balance between dialogue and prose. What needs to be said is said and what isn't, isn't. His characters' conversations are real, not forced, and often serve to make a turn in the plot; they give us glimpses into the possibilities of characters and sometimes foreshadow what is going to happen in the story.

"I think I'm going to call her."

"That's the worst idea you've ever had," Hassan replied immediately. "The. Worst. Idea. Ever."

"No, it's not, because what if she's just waiting for me to call like I'm waiting for her to call?"

"Right, but you're the Dumpee. Dumpees don't call. You know that, *kafir*. Dumpees must never, never call."[16]

Conversations like the above also help elucidate the friendship between the two main characters, Colin and Hassan. It is, in fact, this relationship that clearly outweighs the relationship that Colin is looking for with a Katherine and the one he develops with Lindsey. While Colin struggles to make sense of "love" in a mathematical way, his own friendship with Hassan seems to break all the rules, and that is refreshing. Colin is incredibly smart and somewhat socially awkward. Hassan grounds Colin. He does not let Colin get away with anything, and he speaks the truth, however harsh it might be. He is almost like Colin's conscience. At one point, after Colin has been lying around feeling sorry for himself, Hassan tells him that he needs to stop whining because he hasn't yet become "America's Next Top Genius."[17] He also regularly tells Colin that the stuff Colin knows and wants to throw out into conversation is in no way interesting and will only serve to make him look strange in the eyes of others. Colin understands and appreciates this insight, as he would not have it on his own. Without the development of this relationship, the novel might just be another love story. And certainly it is a love story, but it is also clearly so much more. It is a story that will resonate with all readers, as it has a clear human element; it is a story that will excite readers as they become active participants in its development; and it is a story others will want to tell and remember, and that is what really matters.

NOTES

1. Martha Hamilton and Mitch Weiss, *Children Tell Stories: Teaching and Using Storytelling in the Classroom*, 2nd ed. (Katonah, NY: Richard C. Owen Publishers, 2005), 1.

2. John Green, *An Abundance of Katherines* (New York: Dutton, 2006), 94–95.

3. Ibid., 3.

4. Ibid., 120.

5. Ibid., 202.

6. Ibid., 213.

7. Ibid., 203.

8. Ibid., 63.

9. Ibid., 51.

10. Ibid., 115.
11. Ibid., appendix.
12. Ibid., 119.
13. Ibid., 68, 76, 95.
14. Ibid., 76.
15. Ibid., 8.
16. Ibid., 87.
17. Ibid., 103.

Chapter Six

Paper Towns

Quentin Jacobsen, or Q, is in love with his neighbor, Margo Roth Spiegelman. In fact, he's been in love with her since he was eight years old, and he's not the only one. In fact, everyone has a desire to be with Margo or at least be around her, for there is something special about her, although no one can explain it. Over the years, however, Margo has distanced herself from Q, and the two rarely speak. Still, as a senior in high school, Q holds out for a chance that maybe, someday, they will come back together. Then, suddenly, it appears his greatest wish is coming true, for Margo almost magically appears at his bedroom window, and Q finds himself involved in a crazy all-night adventure that leaves him reeling. But just as quickly as she comes back into his life, Margo suddenly disappears. Despite an impending graduation and finals and the sometimes indifferent attitudes of his best friends, Ben and Radar, Q can't get Margo off his mind. What has happened to her? Where could she be? He makes it his mission to find her, no matter what, and on this journey, he discovers more than he ever imagined.

AN ADOLESCENT'S SEARCH FOR IDENTITY

Ask anyone, and they will probably tell you that adolescents are strange creatures. One minute they are happy and exuberant; the next minute they are moody and sullen. As adults, we often find this fluctuation frustrating, but it is simply a part of growing up. Adolescence is a time of discovery, of trying to find oneself, to uncover and create one's own identity; it is a stormy time. Erik Erikson, in his text *Identity: Youth and Crisis*, describes the adolescence stage in the following way: "The estrangement of this stage is *identity confusion*," in which young people are searching for "a new sense of continuity and sameness" in an effort to eventually find themselves. [1]

John Green centers his novel on this journey of discovery. He captures the mystery that is often involved in finding the self, and in developing this story, he uses techniques that help readers make strong connections, so they can truly see themselves in the text. In fact, the entire novel is about connections—the internal and external connections we make as we grow and develop. Green separates the novel into three sections: "The Strings," "The Grass," and "The Vessel." All of these sections reflect the different stages adolescents work through in their journey of self-discovery.

"The Strings" is the first section of the novel. This section represents the many often-fragile, tenuous connections young people make with others. These are the common things that tie people together, some of which, as one grows and changes, often break. They also represent those initial connections the reader is making with the characters. It is here that we first discover who is involved in the plot.

Green does not go into much physical description of characters. Instead, he focuses on their personalities, quirks, and the relationships they have with others. It is through these elements that we get a clearer picture of them. Even though some characters are described as beautiful, or "honeybunnies," as Ben would call them, there is little else that gives characters a true "face." In essence, Green shows readers that outward appearances don't really matter, not in the end. This forces readers to focus on the inner workings of the characters and become more invested in them as, little by little, they are revealed.

One way Green creates a connection between characters is through their names. Our names help to identify us. We are not abstract formulas or symbols; we are "Tanya Sherwood" or "Steve Klotz." Our names connect us to the past, as they often say something about who we are and where we come from. Green shows the power of names in shaping each character in relation to others—Margo Roth Spiegelman, for example. Throughout the book, she is most often referred to through the use of her full name—first, middle, and last—which gives the character an air of superiority, of majesty. Readers can clearly tell, simply from her name, that she is held to a higher standard: "Margo Roth Spiegelman, whose six-syllable name was often spoken in its entirety with a kind of quiet reverence."[2] Such formality makes her seem above all others, untouchable. After all, celebrities and the like are often given the same courtesy. It's Katy Perry, not Katy; it's Martin Luther King, not Martin. It's the same for Margo. In fact, Q even calls her a "legend." No other character is addressed in such a way, so it is clear that Margo is special. What the reader wants to know, then, is why.

Other characters are given nicknames. These "pseudo names" also help reveal the relationships between the characters and reflect how others view them. Green gives nicknames to three of the significant male characters: Quentin, Ben, and Marcus. These nicknames separate them from all of the other characters at school and define them as part of a particular group. First, there is Quentin, who is simply known as Q. Green does not provide any specifics here, but clearly "Quentin" is a little too formal for his friends, so they shorten his name. Beyond that, however, his friends, Ben specifically, often simply call him "Bro."[3] Once again, this demonstrates the connectedness the boys share. They are like brothers; they share a common bond.

Ben and Q have been best friends since fifth grade, and they know each other like no one else, but Ben's nickname, "Bloody Ben," is one that reflects not this relationship but a different one: "In tenth grade, Ben was hospitalized for a kidney infection, but Becca Arrington, Margo's best friend, started a rumor that the real reason he had blood in his urine was due to chronic masturbation. Despite its medical implausibility, this story had haunted Ben ever since."[4] In this case, Green gives us a clearer picture of how some others view Ben. He is taunted by this nickname, as it is not a true representation of who he is. With young people so often labeling others, this is a connection that may strongly register with many adolescent readers. Even Ben's car has a nickname: RHAPAW. Q describes the car as being "composed primarily out of duct tape and spackle. Her full name was Rode Hard And Put Away Wet, but we called her RHAPAW for short."[5] With other characters driving such vehicles as a Lexus or Chevy Tahoe, this connects Ben to a different grouping, one Q might define as "less socially fortunate."[6]

Next, there is Marcus Lincoln, Q and Ben's best friend. Marcus is only referred to as "Marcus" in the book by his girlfriend, as she is not part of Q's circle of friends. Neither Q nor Ben ever calls him Marcus; instead, he is known as Radar.

> We called him Radar because he looked like a little bespectacled guy
> called Radar on this old TV show M*A*S*H, except 1. The TV Radar

wasn't black, and 2. At some point after the nicknaming, our Radar
grew about six inches and started wearing contacts, so I suppose that 3.
He actually didn't look like the guy on M*A*S*H at all, but 4. With
three and a half weeks left of high school, we weren't very well going to
renickname him.[7]

While some physical descriptions are included, the nicknaming itself still reflects the friendship between the three boys more definitive-
ly.

In addition to naming, there are many other little "strings" Green
slips into the novel that demonstrate characters' journeys as they search
for people and things with which to identify. Q, Ben, and Radar all
share a passion for the video game *Resurrection* and often go to each
other's houses to play. Ben and Radar are both in band, and they both
badly want to go to prom. These are interests not shared with Q. Radar
also has a fascination with Omnictionary, an online reference source,
similar to Wikipedia, on which people can post "factual" information
about a variety of things. Unfortunately, many postings are made, either intentionally or unintentionally, in error. Finding these errors incredibly irritating, Radar makes himself an editor and is constantly
trying to "de-vandalize" postings, an obsession that is his alone.[8]

And then there is one very tenuous string that connects Q and Margo. After being neighbors and childhood friends, the characters' connection has frayed, and they have grown apart; they are no longer
"real" friends. However, when Margo comes back into Q's life for one
night of crazy antics, this string—the one tiny element that binds him
and Margo together—becomes the only string that matters. And it is
through this one night's experiences that Green juxtaposes the two
characters' inner struggles to discover themselves.

Q becomes so engrossed in Margo and her plan for revenge that he
begins to forget himself. Q is not the kind of kid who sneaks out on a
school night, steals his mom's car, or breaks into people's houses, yet
he does all of that just to stay connected to Margo. Even when he is
uncertain why they are doing something, like leaving fish in Margo's
ex-boyfriend's car and in her ex-friend Becca's bed and breaking into
SeaWorld, he can't seem to say no to Margo. He is so in love with her,
calling her "absolutely unprecedented in every way," that no matter
what she asks of him, he will not refuse her.[9] He doesn't want the night
with her to end, so he keeps her talking as much as possible and tries to

impress her by being the person he believes she wants him to be. This marks the beginning of Q losing his identity in Margo.

Margo, on the other hand, begins breaking her strings. To her, the whole evening of mayhem is about cutting ties to people she no longer wants to be associated with: "Just, God. I just hate myself so much for even caring about my, quote, friends. I mean, just so you know, it's not that I am oh-so-upset about Jason. Or Becca. Or even Lacey, although I actually liked her. But it was the last string. It was a lame string, for sure, but it was the one I had left." [10] Instead of forming connections, she is beginning to move away from all of those things, those people who apparently bind her. She wants to be her own person, without the pressures put upon her by others. Q, however, is blind to this. He only sees that he still has a connection with Margo, and he wants to keep that for as long as possible. And when Margo disappears, this connection becomes all the more important.

In "The Grass," the second section of Green's novel, the focus shifts to a different facet of adolescents' search for identity, one in which teens essentially lose themselves in another. Erikson explains, "To keep themselves together they temporarily overidentify with the heroes of cliques and crowds to the point of an apparently complete loss of individuality." [11] Once again, Green shows the reader two sides of this through the development of characters: Q, who loses himself in Margo, and Margo, who simply wants to lose herself.

In *Leaves of Grass*, Walt Whitman expresses the fact that we are all connected. We come from the earth, and we eventually return to the earth and become part of it. Thus, in a sense, we become the grass. This demonstrates the depth of Q's connection to Margo once she disappears. Q looks for her everywhere and sees her in everything. He feels her out there, and he becomes obsessed with finding her. "Margo's mom had said that Margo's clues never led anywhere, but I knew now that Margo had created a chain of clues—and she had seemingly made them for me." [12] No longer is it just a small string that binds him to her; it is his whole being. In looking at her in such a "large" way, Q's focus on school, his friends, and his family becomes skewed. He rearranges his life, takes risks he never would have, and gives up his own graduation in order to find her. He begins to lose his connections to others in an effort to keep his connection with Margo, even in the smallest of ways. He gets angry at Ben because he won't help look for Margo and begins to question their friendship. And as his search for clues to Margo's whereabouts intensifies, he becomes more and more disappointed with Lacey and Radar as well, as neither one demonstrates the same fervent interest. Q is so absorbed in his own journey that he wants everyone to stop their lives and join him, as though his quest is so much more important than everyone else's.

As things progress in the search, Q does begin to make some realizations, however. He slowly recognizes that he has created this image of Margo that might not be real. "All along—not only since she left, but for a decade before—I had been imagining her without listening, without knowing that she made as poor a window as I did. . . . And all at once I knew how Margo Roth Spiegelman felt when she wasn't being Margo Roth Spiegelman: She felt empty."[13]

Still, Q cannot give up on his quest to find Margo. He is certain she wants him to find her and that she is out there waiting for him. He believes he knows her as well as she knows herself.

Erikson wrote about adolescents, "They are sometimes morbidly, often curiously, preoccupied with what they appear to be in the eyes of others as compared with what they feel they are."[14] This has been Margo's trap. Unlike Q, who gives up his own individuality in his search for Margo, Margo struggles to let go of what others want or expect her to be. Everyone sees her as this amazing person who does these crazy things no one else would ever do, simply because she is Margo Roth Spiegelman. She is seen as a hero, as someone to look up to, and as someone to admire and to put on a pedestal: "Margo Roth Spiegelman, whose stories of epic adventures would blow through school like a summer storm: an old guy living in a broken-down house in Hot Coffee, Mississippi, taught Margo how to play the guitar. Margo Roth Spiegelman, who drank a cup of herbal tea with The Mallionaires backstage after a concert in St. Louis while they drank whiskey."[15]

She is like Superman to her classmates, but just as it was for Clark Kent, it is only a costume. Nobody really knows Margo; they only know their interpretation of who she is. They only see her from their own perspective. At one point, Lacey and Q discuss the fact that Margo might be dead: "'That doesn't sound like my Margo,' she said, and I thought of my Margo, and Lacey's Margo, and Mrs. Spiegelman's Margo, and all of us looking at her reflection in different fun house mirrors."[16] And that's it: none of them really see Margo for who she is; they see what they want to see, often something they lack in themselves.

Interestingly, Margo's parents see her in a completely different way. They see her as a self-centered, immature teenager who has no consideration for others. She has run away from home in the past, and her parents, because they do not understand her or her behavior, are "done" with her. Her father, instead of responding with worry to Margo's disappearance, responds with relief. He refers to her as "a sickness"—something that has invaded their home and made their lives miserable.[17] Her mother responds similarly, noting that they have another child to think about, so they can't be spending their time worrying about Margo anymore. It seems Margo is not, nor perhaps has ever been, a true part of the family. By removing Margo from the novel early on, Green actually gives readers a better understanding of her and the difficulty in creating one's own identity. So often, we try to live up to others' expectations, but it is simply not possible. Each person has to live for himself or herself, and by the end of the novel, that is what the characters finally begin to uncover.

The last section of the novel is entitled "The Vessel." In this section, Green focuses on the characters as individuals. They are finally beginning to see each other for who they really are. In the adolescent's search for self, this is the final phase: to finally break free and stand alone. As Erikson points out, "In the social jungle of human existence there is no feeling of being alive without a sense of identity."[18]

The strings and the grass—the connections—are still there, yet it is this image of the vessel that becomes the one of the individual. Early in the novel, Q refers to Margo as a vessel: "In the end, you could not say that Margo Roth Spiegelman was fat, or that she was skinny, any more than you can say that the Eiffel Tower is or is not lonely. Margo's beauty was a kind of sealed vessel of perfection—uncracked and uncrackable."[19] It isn't until after Q finds Margo, however, that he realizes it's not really "her"; she isn't the Margo he had in his mind. She never really wanted him to find her. She did want to be alone, to escape. And suddenly he realizes his first interpretation of a vessel was all wrong: there is no perfection. Each person is just who he or she is and nothing more.

Q finally realizes he cannot change his life and give up his own identity for Margo. Margo wants to get away, wants to travel and be more than "an idea that everybody likes."[20] But Q sees things differently: "The thing is, I do believe in college, and jobs, and maybe even babies one day. I do believe in the future."[21] He has his own desires, his own wants, and he needs to fulfill them. He comes to grips with who he really is and who he isn't, and he knows he cannot follow Margo any longer. In the end, Q's search for Margo becomes his own search for identity, and when he finds her, he ultimately finds himself.

NOTES

1. Erik Erikson, *Identity: Youth and Crisis* (New York: Norton, 1968), 111, 114.
2. John Green, *Paper Towns* (New York: Dutton, 2008), 14.
3. Ibid.
4. Ibid., 13.
5. Ibid., 90.
6. Ibid., 97.
7. Ibid., 12.
8. Ibid., 15.
9. Ibid., 31.
10. Ibid., 58.
11. Erikson, *Identity*, 132.
12. Green, *Paper Towns*, 113.
13. Ibid., 199.
14. Erikson, *Identity*, 128.
15. Green, *Paper Towns*, 115.
16. Ibid., 185.
17. Ibid., 131.
18. Erikson, *Identity*, 130.
19. Green, *Paper Towns*, 50.
20. Ibid., 294.
21. Ibid., 295.

Chapter Seven

The Indifference of the Universe

The fault, dear Brutus, is not in our stars / But in ourselves.
—William Shakespeare, *Julius Caesar*

In a perfect world, two people fall in mad, passionate love and live happily ever after. In a perfect world, loss is a myth. In a perfect world, the stars align and promise happiness. The world, however, is far from perfect, and we must navigate our way through the indifferent and sometimes cruel universe.

The Fault in Our Stars opens with a young girl named Hazel Grace Lancaster who is looking back on the winter of her seventeenth year, a year when she lives more than all of her previous years combined. This novel *is* about living: living with love, living with loss, and living with what the fates have designed. Hazel is a cancer survivor, with lungs that suck at being lungs. By doctor's orders, and her mother's prodding, Hazel attends a cancer support group. "Fights were recounted, battles won amid wars sure to be lost; hope was clung to; families were both celebrated and denounced; it was agreed that friends just didn't get it; tears were shed; comfort proffered." [1]

This support group, which meets weekly, is comprised of kids battling various types—at varying stages—of cancer. Led by Peter, a cancer survivor himself, this group seeks to provide an outlet for these young people. Hazel is quick to mock the routine of the meetings and Peter's attempts to make the teenagers see hope in what is often a hopeless situation. She is annoyed with what she calls "the circle jerk of support" [2] until she meets *him*: Augustus Waters. Ridiculously handsome and hilariously witty, Augustus invites Hazel into his world of possibility—a world where she is able to feel a semblance of normalcy, a world where she falls in love, and a world where she learns that the stars just might have finally aligned.

THE PLAYERS—NOT NECESSARILY IN THE ORDER THEY ARE INTRODUCED

All the world's a stage, and all the men and women merely players.
—William Shakespeare, *As You Like It*

Kaitlyn

Kaitlyn just happened to be an extremely sophisticated twenty-five-year-old British socialite stuck inside a sixteen-year-old body in Indianapolis. [3]

Hazel wasn't always sick. At one point in her life, she was a normal, healthy child with normal, healthy friends. Kaitlyn is that friend. The complete opposite of Hazel, Kaitlyn is the epitome of a teenager. She is dramatic. She shops voraciously. And she adopts a vernacular all her own and miles away from Indianapolis where she lives. Hazel maintains their friendship, but there is an obvious elephant in the room when they meet. Cancer has driven a wedge, but Kaitlyn remains Hazel's go-to for advice about fashion and relationships.

Isaac

His eyes were the problem. He had some fantastically improbable eye cancer. One eye had been cut out when he was a kid . . . a recurrence had placed his remaining eye in mortal peril. [4]

The first cancer friend introduced in the novel is Isaac. In fact it is Isaac who introduces Hazel and Augustus. Suffering from cancer of the eyes, Isaac wears thick glasses to provide a semblance of visibility in the one eye he has left. Midway through the novel he sacrifices his other eye, a surgery that yields NEC (no evidence of cancer). This sacrifice reminds us that "pain demands to be felt." [5] To compound the misery of his physical sacrifice, his girlfriend Monica breaks his heart when she can't seem to "handle" dating someone with cancer. What is especially interesting about this relationship, however, is that John Green initially portrays the two lovers as passionately "into" each other for "always." Isaac's "always" ends much sooner than anticipated, however, and the reader is left feeling anger and empathy. Through Hazel, Green says, "Well, to be fair, I mean, she probably *can't* handle it. Neither can you, but she doesn't *have* to handle it and you do."[6] And so it goes that Monica can't *handle* Isaac's illness and Isaac can't *handle* Monica's betrayal. Isaac reminds us that pain is indeed very demanding.

Hazel

> There is only one thing in this world shittier than biting it from cancer when you're sixteen, and that's having a kid who bites it from cancer.[7]

Hazel "Grace" Lancaster is a cancer miracle. She has purchased a bit of time due to an experimental drug with a very low chance of success. Honest and endearing, this young protagonist reminds the reader to appreciate life's blessings and to seize every day of life. Hazel is a vegetarian, in hopes of minimizing the amount of death for which she is responsible, and she is never without Philip, her oxygenator. The honesty with which she illustrates the plight of a cancer patient is not only insightful but also inspirational. Hazel Grace is a daughter constantly reminded of the burden cancer places upon her parents, a friend constantly mindful of the necessity to choose among truths, a girlfriend constantly conscious of the ugliness of her disease, and a mortal constantly trying to defy the odds.

Augustus

> I liked the way his story ended with someone else. I liked his voice. I liked that he was a tenured professor in the Department of Slightly Crooked Smiles with a dual appointment in the Department of Having a Voice that Made My Skin Feel More Like Skin.[8]

It is only fitting that a young, terminally ill girl—albeit miraculously remitted—encounters the man of her dreams in a cancer support group. Augustus is a Greek Adonis who smokes because he refuses to empower the cancer causer, who drives with a prosthetic right leg, and who rescues the young from predators paying the price of dawn (the price of which is blood) in the similarly titled video game. Hazel is the "grenade" holding the potential to destroy those in her path, and Augustus is the "side effect" of this horrific disease. This side effect, however, changes the course of Hazel's existence. He is handsome, he is witty, and he is buying time in a world that often charges too high a price. When Hazel catches Augustus's glance, she finally understands the phrase "*eye contact*"; she is smitten and the reader cannot help but be smitten as well. Augustus is larger than life. He is the bright spot in a life filled with darkness, and he instills a sense of hope into a hopeless situation.

Once a star basketball player, Augustus loses his ability to play when his leg gets amputated due to his bout with osteosarcoma. He is in remission when the novel begins, and his sacrifice seems small because of his larger-than-life presence. His humor is contagious, and the reader rallies behind this young man who uses his "wish" to make Hazel's dreams come true.

The Parents

A frail father who cannot bear the thought of his little girl dying, an angry mother who cannot fathom letting her dying son leave for even a few days, and distant siblings who cannot even attempt to understand the shell of a person who replaced their dying brother are all representative of the fact that the family grieves too.

What is especially honest about the way Green portrays the family members is his description of their shades of grief. The reader meets parents who, while they are hyper-aware of their terminally ill children, try to maintain a sense of normalcy through daily celebrations of hope. Hazel's mother celebrates holidays that only calendars know about, half birthdays and anniversaries, and life in general. When she accompanies Hazel and Augustus to Amsterdam, she gives them the privacy for this budding romance to bloom. And at the end of the novel, she reveals her desire to counsel others. Hazel's mother embodies the reciprocity of loss. We lose. We grieve. We give back. We find a way to remain true to the legacy of our own suffering.

Likewise, Augustus's parents are models of normality despite their struggle with their son's illness. When they first meet Hazel, they welcome her into their fold of "Encouragements." These motivating aphorisms, "cross-stitched sentiments" of hope, are strategically placed all over Augustus's home. The reader is both amused and moved by these genuine, albeit rather cheesy, gestures of support. Augustus's parents embrace the budding romance between the two, and Hazel becomes a permanent fixture in their household as the novel draws to a close. Parents in young adult novels are often rather disconnected to the adolescents. Green, however, furthers the emotional impact of the events in the novel by making the reader aware that these young people, so unjustly affected by the faulty stars, are indeed loved and cherished.

CAN WE RECONCILE THE IRRECONCILABLE?

The robbed that smiles steals something from the thief.
—William Shakespeare, *Othello*

Green's argument about the indifference of the universe and our ability or lack thereof to remain hopeful is the crux of this novel. What is especially moving about these young characters afflicted with this capricious disease is their ability to find humor and hope amidst a physical world that offers little. They reconcile the irreconcilable, and the reader is left inspired and in awe of their courage while questioning the justness of the universe.

Aside from the physical battle that each of the young characters in the novel faces, there is a mental struggle to reconcile and understand the strange and often cruel twists of fate. The characters expose the very raw nature of cancer, and at times, the reader is left smirking through sadness. This juxtaposition of contrasting emotions is an indication of the reader's struggle to come to terms with the unfairness of cancer. Green, in a statement on his website, argues that this struggle manifests not only philosophically but also in our daily struggles to "try to live full, productive lives." And thus the characters often reconcile their situations through experiences and conversations unique to cancer patients.

When Hazel first broaches the topic of cancer perks, something Green dubs "the little things cancer kids get that regular kids don't," there is a sense of irony. Regular kids *don't* get cancer and so they miss out on the perks: the autographs, celebrity visits, and such. They trade life for memorabilia—a tough bargain. While Green has to explain the concept of the cancer perk to the reader, Augustus is well aware of what they are.

This unspoken understanding and communication unique to cancer patients appears throughout the novel. Both Hazel and Augustus have selected their death attire, something many of us cannot fathom. The conversation happens at the beginning of what turns out to be the most romantic night of their lives. Again, the reader is jolted by the cancer patient's world. We are horrified by the prospect of adolescents selecting the clothing with which they will be laid to rest, but at the same time we are in awe of their courage for doing so.

ARE THERE DEGREES OF SUFFERING?

With a book jacket that uses words like "terminal," "tragic," "devastating," and "diagnosis," the reader can't help but anticipate that suffering will play a large role in this novel. What is exceptional about this novel, however, is that there are degrees of suffering that we are forced to recognize. Hazel chronicles these degrees the first night of support group. When we discover Isaac will lose his other eye, there is sadness and empathy for his suffering. And yet, he rationalizes the loss of his sight by acknowledging that others have it worse. Augustus, while physically beautiful, suffered a "little touch" of osteosarcoma resulting in the sacrifice of a leg. Lida, a survivor of appendiceal cancer, greatly admires Hazel's will to fight, an admiration reciprocated by Hazel with envy toward Lida's remission. And there's Michael, a twelve-year-old leukemia patient, who eventually loses his battle with cancer. The degrees of sacrifice are staggering, and yet "all salvation is temporary,"[9] an affirmation that helps the reader find meaning in each character's suffering. It is awful. It is unfair. But it has meaning.

Green confronts this notion of meaning head-on in this novel. The suffering and unjust nature of this disease is unavoidable. The challenge, however, lies not in the suffering but in the search for hope. Each of the characters, survivors or not, embody perseverance. Isaac blindly navigates the labyrinth in *The Price of Dawn* video game; Augustus rescues the innocent so they can live another day; Hazel bequeaths her swing set, the ultimate metaphor of her health and youth, to a deserving family; and they all engage in the cathartic smashing of his trophies following Isaac's surgery and sacrifice of his eye. While cancer is ever present in their lives, these adolescents manage to prevail over their misery.

CAN WE BELIEVE IN TEENAGE LOVE?

Love is often viewed as an emotion that cannot be felt by anybody other than adults. Phrases like "puppy love" are used to describe this powerful attraction between adolescents. Green, however, makes the reader believe differently. When Hazel first sees Augustus, she is "suddenly conscious of [her] myriad of insufficiencies,"[10] she begins to grasp to meaning of "eye contact," and from this magnetic attraction she acknowledges that falling in love with someone terminally ill is destined for heartbreak. Hazel is constantly reminded of her responsibilities as a daughter and a girlfriend. She recognizes the implications of her roles, and while the first is a circumstance of birth, the latter is a role she resists. Intimacy yields heartbreak, and Hazel wants to avoid causing any more damage to those who love her. She is willing to sacrifice her happiness to avoid hurting Augustus. That is love.

Likewise, Augustus is drawn to Hazel. He relentlessly pursues her company, he reads her beloved "best book ever," and he uses his own final wish to make her dreams of traveling to Amsterdam come true. Unlike Hazel, however, Augustus is eager to involve himself in a romantic relationship. He embodies love and sacrifice, and he is impossible to resist. When Hazel tries to isolate herself, he finds a way to engage her. He reminds her of what it feels like to live and helps her forget her disease. That is love.

What is especially notable about Hazel and Augustus's relationship is that they don't have to profess their love in order for it to be real. They are young, yes. But they are old souls. And thus their actions, their gestures, and their closeness are more intimate than any words. "Okay." One word says it all: they are okay and they are in love.

> Life's but a walking shadow, a poor player that struts and frets his hour
> upon the stage and then is heard no more: it is a tale told by an idiot, full
> of sound and fury, signifying nothing.
> —William Shakespeare, *Macbeth*

AIA—AN IMPERIAL AFFLICTION, PETER VAN HOUSEN

Cancer is an unforgiving, nondiscriminatory disease. It attacks and we are left wondering why. When it strikes the young, however, we are left searching for reasons, often seeking solace elsewhere. Hazel finds solace in a book called *An Imperial Affliction*. *AIA* is about a young girl named Anna who lives in central California until she gets a rare blood cancer. Hazel is quick to defend her choice of reading, claiming that it IS NOT a cancer book. Rather, she is drawn to Anna because she is honest in a way that few are. The book is a stroke of literary genius, according to Hazel. It ends in the middle of a sentence, and Hazel seeks answers to the questions the novel leaves: "I understood the story ended . . . and this midsentence thing was supposed to reflect how life really ends and whatever, but there were characters other than Anna in the story, and it seemed unfair that I would never find out what happened to them."[11]

When she shares the novel with Augustus, he too sees its allure and feels it is important. The two reach out to contact Peter Van Housen, the author. They begin to correspond, and the contact leads to a trip to Amsterdam where the adolescents meet this larger-than-life literary mogul.

Green writes Van Housen through the eyes of Hazel, and at first the reader is led to believe that he is worthy of her affections. But when she meets him, those sentiments change. The man, "duly impressed by the Shakespearean complexity of [her] tragedy,"[12] is a bitter, reclusive alcoholic. He is verbally abusive to both Hazel and Augustus, and the reader is inclined to despise him. But after further development, he is seen as a sad shell of a man, an idiot who tells a tale signifying little.

While *AIA* ends midsentence, *The Fault in Our Stars* does not. Augustus writes a letter to Van Housen requesting that this "shitty person" but "great writer" pen a eulogy for Hazel. What follows however is a beautiful eulogy written by Augustus in the form of this request. So yes, the writer afflicted Hazel with his book, but it was Augustus's love that sent the message.

There will come a time when all of us are dead. All of us.
—Hazel Lancaster[13]

NOTES

1. John Green, *The Fault in Our Stars* (New York: Penguin, 2012), 12.
2. Ibid., 11.
3. Ibid., 42.
4. Ibid., 6.
5. Ibid., 57.
6. Ibid., 60.
7. Ibid., 8.
8. Ibid., 32.

9. Ibid., 59.
10. Ibid., 9.
11. Ibid., 50.
12. Ibid., 112.
13. Ibid., 12.

Chapter Eight

Nerdfighters! John Green Style

John Green and Hank Green's wildly popular ning website, Nerdfighters.com, proclaims the Green brothers' mission "to fight to increase awesome and decrease suck."[1] Extending the Nerdfighters' superhero/martial arts metaphor, "awesome" and "suck" easily stand in for good and evil. In fact, characterizing Green's style as a novelist is a little like describing the superhero/martial arts legend Bruce Lee (Kato in *The Green Hornet*), whose fighting style, Jeet Kune Do, was often characterized as simple, smooth, and direct. John Green's simple and direct writing style fights to illuminate the good in life, even when that good may amount to fleeting moments in the life of a terminally ill teen.

At the same time, Green refuses to obsess over the negative, no matter how bad a character's situation. Winner of nearly every major book award there is for young adult literature, this author definitely increases awesome and decreases suck in the lives of young (and old) readers. But teen readers can spot a phony Dewey Decimal System right away, and they reject Pollyannas for not respecting the emotional complexity of their lives. Green's stories include death, alienation, and all the pain that goes with them, but somehow he draws readers in while refusing to dip his plots in angst. How does he do that?

Stephen Roxburgh, founder of Front Street Books and former senior vice president of Farrar, Straus, and Giroux, once characterized the most important nuance of young adult literature as voice, correctly pointing out that the tendency for decades has been to classify young adult literature by audience and/or point of view, which we do not use to classify other genres of literature. Roxburgh says that "character is made manifest in and by the protagonist's voice."[2] Green is nothing if not a master of adolescent voice: voice in narration and voice in dialogue. The Northwest Regional Educational Laboratory, which holds the copyright on a model called the Six Traits of Writing, defines voice as "the writer coming through the words, the sense that a real person is speaking to us . . . . a personal tone and flavor . . . . that individual something."[3] In any Green novel, readers get the undeniable sense that a teenager is talking to them.

The key to teen voice, whether in a narrator or character, lies in understanding adolescent psychology. Through years of research both on behavior and brain development, adolescent psychologists have come to place particular emphasis on the teen years as a time of exploration, autonomy seeking, and risk taking. As Dr. Marilyn Price-Mitchell explains in *Psychology Today*, "Changes to the limbic system of the brain cause teens to seek risk, challenge, and emotional stimulation."[4] Adolescence is a time of emotional vulnerability. Teens simultaneously fear being different from everyone else and failing to be unique. They seek the society of their peers and yet can be cruelly exclusive and fearful of the other.

Autonomy and risk taking are central to the most powerful young adult novels, and although Green surely captures the rhythm, tone, and emotion of the adolescent voice in general, he does much more. The narrators and characters don't just sound like adolescents, they *feel* like adolescents. He uses voice to manifest the essence of the teen years on the quest for self-determination, capturing all of the accompanying characteristics and contradictions adolescents demonstrate, including eagerness, uncertainty, ambiguity, a degree of innocence, hopefulness, and sometimes alienation. Typically, protagonists in Green's novels take some sort of journey, figuratively or literally, arriving at a new school, a new place, a new group, a new situation, a new experience, or some alignment of their stars that makes "risk, challenge, and emotional stimulation" almost unavoidable as they seek to regain their equilibrium and achieve autonomy. In this way, the stage is set for the adolescent voice Green so artfully creates, a voice that makes identification with his characters so easy and appealing. Readers inhabit the characters, especially the protagonist, subconsciously, because the situations, as interpreted in an adolescent voice, call out to them.

Adolescence means self-consciousness to the level of hyperawareness. Green's characters never fail to anguish over how they look.

Adolescent anguish over appearance is constantly evident in *Will Grayson, Will Grayson*, the story of two young men in Chicago with the same name, whose paths accidently cross, coauthored by John Green and David Levithan. Levithan writes the chapters told from the point of view of one will grayson, who lives in Naperville, Illinois, has an absentee father, and is gay. Green writes the chapters told from the perspective of the other eponymous Will Grayson, who lives in Evanston, and whose best friend Tiny Cooper is about to put on a play about the trials and tribulations of being Tiny Cooper, a giant football player who is very artistic and also gay. No one is more aware of how others see his physical self than Tiny. Tiny's voice, although emanating from a giant body, smacks of adolescent vulnerability as he talks with gay will grayson about his outsized body (absence of capitals indicates which Will Grayson is telling the story):

> What really gets to me—what *really* bothers me—is that it's all people see. ever since I was a not-so-little kid. *Hey, tiny, want to play football? hey, tiny, how many burgers did you eat today? you ever lose your dick down there? hey, tiny, you're going to join the basketball team whether you like it or not. just don't try to look at us in the locker room!* does that sound easy to you, will?[5]

Despite claims to the contrary about loving his own body, Tiny craves approval by his peers and hopes the play will convey to the world how it feels to be Tiny Cooper.

Being cool is everything, but coping with not being cool is even better. Green provides a sort of antihero coping mechanism in which characters often cope with their perceived inadequacies through a sort of self-deprecating humor, reminiscent of adult authors (if you can call them that) David Sedaris, Dave Barry, and Bill Bryson. When *Looking for Alaska* protagonist Miles Halter first arrives at Culver Creek private boarding school, his new roommate Chip "the Colonel" Martin immediately gives him the nickname "Pudge . . . because you're skinny. It's called irony, Pudge. Heard of it?"[6] The Colonel proceeds to explain the Culver Creek caste system, telling Miles that there are the rich Birmingham "cool kids" who "go home to their parents' air-conditioned mansions every weekend" and look down their noses at "the regular boarders" like him.[7] Apparently, Miles has not been living on the cutting edge of fashion because his low-slung, baggy shorts become a running gag for the first few days of school, a fashion faux pas that suggests to the Colonel that Miles is a public, not a private, school kid who may think himself to be "hot shit." Miles's reaction is typical Green: "I wore my shorts just below my hips, which I thought was cool. Finally, I said, 'Yeah, I went to public school. But I wasn't hot shit, Chip. I was regular shit.'"[8] Sometimes "regular shit" is the best a teen can aspire to.

Another example of coping with the embarrassment of adolescence through self-deprecating humor occurs in *An Abundance of Katherines*, even though the story is not told in first person. In the story, our protagonist, Colin, has been once again rejected by yet another girl named Katherine, making nineteen in all. Colin imagines his failed love life plotted out along a bell curve showing all romantic involvements around the world in terms of whether individuals have been rejected ("dumped") or done the rejecting ("dumpees").[9] The perfect bell curve displayed on page 16 displays that in any and all romantic rejections, half of the people fall on one side of the median, showing the majority of the population to have a fairly even distribution between being dumped and doing the dumping—but not Colin and his Katherines. The nineteen Katherines fall spot on the axis for always being the dumpers, and Colin falls spot on the axis for being the dumpee. He is a perfect loser, but graphing it out like an eleventh-grade geometry story problem makes it funny, and the humor makes it less painful, something Colin can live with.

The adolescent voice is constantly evident in *Will Grayson, Will Grayson*. This book is mostly internal dialogue, conversations, and text messages rather than narration of action, making it prime for voice. As Green sets the stage for the conflict and characters, readers are clued in on how his Evanston Will Grayson copes with the uncertainties of a Facebook conversation with the crush he cannot admit to, Jane Turner:

> I have the distinct feeling that flirting is occurring. Now, don't get me wrong. I enjoy flirting as much as the next guy, provided that the next guy has repeatedly seen his best friend torn asunder by love. But nothing violates the rules of shutting up and not caring so much as flirting— except possibly that enchantingly horrible moment when you act upon the flirting, that moment when you seal your heartbreak with a kiss. There should be a third rule, actually: 1. Shut up. 2. Don't care too much. And 3. Never kiss a girl you like.[10]

Before the novel is over, and in almost every chapter, Will Grayson sustains a voice that will deeply resonate with most adolescents and call out to anyone who has ever been in love, self-conscious, rejected by a friend, or lost a romantic interest to someone older and more worldly.

Sarcasm is as much a teen modus operandi as eye rolling and scowling, and in the hands of a deft user it can be a form of coping through humor. Adolescence can be a time of feeling powerless, and nothing evokes the feeling more than having a terminal illness. As Green's *Fault in Our Stars* sets the cast of characters, readers meet Isaac, who is losing his eyes to cancer:

> Okay, so I went into the clinic this morning, and I was telling my surgeon that I'd rather be deaf than blind, and he said, "It doesn't work that way," and I was like, "Yeah, I realize it doesn't work that way; I'm just saying I'd rather be deaf than blind if I had the choice, which I realize that I don't have," and he said, "Well, the good news is you won't be deaf," and I was like, "Thank you for explaining that my eye cancer isn't going to make me deaf. I feel so fortunate that an intellectual giant like yourself would deign to operate on me." [11]

Sometimes not even self-deprecation and sarcasm can save a teen from being uncool. In the matter of autonomy, another one of adolescence's embarrassing factors can be parents. In *Paper Towns*, Marcus "Radar" Lincoln is so embarrassed by his parents that he refuses to take his girlfriend, Angela, to his house. The narrator and protagonist Quentin "Q" Jacobsen explains that Radar's parents are in the *Guinness Book of Records*, although readers don't know why until this exchange on the subject among Q, Ben, and Radar:

> "Seriously, bro," added Ben. "She's a really nice girl. I don't see why you can't introduce her to your parents and show her Casa Radar."
>
> Radar threw his books into his locker and shut it. The din of conversation around us quieted just a bit as he turned his eyes toward the heavens and shouted, "IT IS NOT MY FAULT THAT MY PARENTS OWN THE WORLD'S LARGEST COLLECTION OF BLACK SANTAS." [12]

Adolescent voice can be about frustration but also about uncertainty and ambiguity. In *Will Grayson, Will Grayson*, Green articulates the thoughts and conversations of his awkward protagonist and champion screwup, Will, who puts together words in ironic ways that perfectly reflect his contradictory frame of mind. In regard to the rock band Maybe Dead Cats, Will says, "I kind of absolutely love them." [13] Grayson's feelings also take contradictory stances when it comes to Jane Turner, who has made it perfectly clear she is interested in him. His heart, brain, and mouth are disconnected somehow, and as he talks with her on the phone, he realizes how confused he is and what a mess he is making of everything: "I want her. I don't. I have no idea what to say, so I go ahead and say the worst possible thing."[14]

One of Green's stylistic tricks to convey the out-of-control schizophrenic feeling of adolescence is the run-on sentence. Although Will Grayson claims to be ambivalent on the whole subject of Jane, he obviously obsesses over her, placing disproportionate weight on the choice of every word he uses with her. When he describes a note she wrote him as "cute," Jane appears offended. His best friend, Tiny Cooper, commiserates:

> I ask him if he agrees with me about what the end of her sentence probably was, and then I ask him what shortcircuited in my brain to call the note cute, and how is it even possible to be both attracted and not attracted to someone at the very same time, and whether or not I am a robot incapable of real feelings, and do you think that actually, like, trying to follow the rules about shutting up and not caring has made me into some kind of hideous monster whom no one will ever marry.[15]

This sentence is nearly one hundred words long, and we can imagine Will gasping for breath in between clauses but refusing to stop until he had expressed all his feelings. The run-on-sentence technique perfectly represents the flood of emotions pouring out in an adolescent voice.

Another technique Green uses is repeating a quick, choppy cadence. About two-thirds of the way through *Looking for Alaska*, on page 139 of 221, Miles expresses his shock over the principal's sobbing revelation that Alaska Young has been killed instantly in a car accident.

> I thought: *It's all my fault.*
> I thought: *I don't feel very good.*
> I thought: *I'm going to throw up.*

Generally, adolescents are ill prepared to deal with death, especially the death of a close peer whom they love, and Miles loved Alaska. Green continues the rapid-fire voice, as Miles vacillates from stark realization to physical illness and euphoric denial: "She's not dead. She's alive. She's alive somewhere. She's in the woods. Alaska is hiding in the woods, and she's not dead, she's just hiding. She's just playing a trick on us."[16]

On a lighter note, the adolescent developmental need for "risk, challenge, and emotional stimulation" can lead to some envelope pushing. They experiment with behaviors they previously perceived to be inappropriate and off limits. According to adolescent psychologist Lawrence Kohlberg, people go through stages of moral reasoning.[17] They move from conforming to society's rules for behavior without question to deciding for themselves whether their behavior will be based, not on fear of punishment from authority, but on their own abstract reasoning. Teens venturing into these stages of abstract moral reasoning who experiment with this envelope pushing are also learning that rule violation can have unforeseen consequences. Green's characters act out what adolescent readers would like to do themselves, but experiencing it vicariously through fiction is definitely safer.

Risk taking may lead to inappropriate/objectionable language choices, a practice that may or may not lose its appeal as adolescence winds down but is definitely a part of the culture. Testicle references of all kinds and "your mom" references of a sexual nature are common among teenage boys. In their peer group, making these remarks may be considered a sign of masculinity and being offended by them just the opposite. Inappropriate behavior can also be a means of venting. Unpopular teachers and classes may be on the receiving end of these references, as in *Paper Towns* when Radar expresses his dislike for his government class to Q, who changes the topic to Radar's girlfriend, Angela:

> "I just decided during government that I would actually, literally suck donkey balls if it meant I could skip that class for the rest of the semester," he said.
> "You can learn a lot about government from donkey balls," I said.
> "Hey, speaking of reasons you wish you had fourth-period lunch, we just dined with Angela."[18]

When Q's mother kisses him on the cheek as she drops him off at school, Q's close friend Ben makes inappropriate sexual remarks about Q's mom, elbows him in the ribs, but doesn't give it a second thought.[19]

Adolescent voice in all its inappropriateness, humorous as it may be, even permeates what is probably the saddest of Green's novels, *The Fault in Our Stars*, the story of two terminally ill teens, Hazel and Augustus (Gus), who fall in love. Sixteen-year-old Hazel is saddened by the swing set in her backyard, about which she has many happy memories, but that is now abandoned, rusting, and weed choked. Under a gray sky, she sits in the backyard, crying and entertaining memories of her father putting it together for her when she was small. She calls Gus, who comes right over to see what he can do. He decides they should give it away, and they set out to write an ad for a website called "Free No Catch":

> "Headline?" he asked.
>   "Swing Set Needs Home," I said.
>   "Desperately Lonely Swing Set Needs Loving Home," he said.
>   "Lonely, Vaguely Pedophilic Swing Set Seeks the Butts of Children," I said.
>   He laughed. "That's why."
>   "What?"
>   "That's why I like you."[20]

Sometimes it helps just to be inappropriately silly.

It can also help sometimes to use inappropriate language when feelings run too deep to express without a little creative swearing. In *An Abundance of Katherines*, Colin's friend Hassan has been providing emotional succor to him for years as Colin went through nineteen breakups with nineteen different Katherines, but Hassan finally gets sick of being taken for granted by his best friend. Many a teen probably wishes they had found the nerve to say exactly what Green has Hassan say:

> And then Hassan lost it.
>   "Has it ever crossed your mind, you ungrateful asshole, that when I was mopping up after all your breakups, when I was picking your sorry ass off the floor of your bedroom, when I was listening to your endless rantings and ravings about every fugging girl who ever gave you the time of day, that maybe I was actually doing it for you and not to learn of the newest dumping in your life? What problems have you listened to of mine, dillhole? Have you ever sat with me for hours and listened to me whine about being a fat fugger whose best friend ditches him every time a new Katherine comes along?"[21]

People of all ages feel unappreciated by their friends at times, but for teens it can be a devastating reoccurring heartache. Like Lawrence Kohlberg, psychologist Erik Erikson also projects a series of human developmental stages.[22] As adolescents approach the end of their teen years, they reach what Erikson calls "young adulthood," at which time he says that they are entering the stage of readiness for "intimacy." Without successful, strong relationships, young adults experience "loneliness and isolation."[23] After Green's character Will Grayson has been trying to sort out the painful feelings he has been experiencing, he finally figures out that the reason he cannot yet pursue a healthful relationship with Jane, and the reason he is so depressed, is that he feels abandoned by the fellow who has been his best friend as far back as he can remember. He loves his best friend Tiny, not in a sexual way, but as the person he has most counted on in life. Will goes to their special sanctuary, the public park baseball dugout where Tiny stood up for Will when they were little boys, hoping that Tiny will find him so he can tell him how he feels. And he does. Will lets him have it:

"You are a terrible best friend," I tell him. "Terrible!" You totally ditch me every time you have a new boyfriend, and then you come crawling back when you're heartbroken. You don't listen to me. You don't even seem to *like* me. You get obsessed with the play and totally ignore me except to insult me to our friend behind my back, and you exploit your life and the people you say you care about so that your little play can make people love you and think how awesome you are and how liberated you are, how wondrously gay you are, but you know what? Being gay is not an excuse for being a dick.[24]

At this point the novel is approaching its climax, and the problem of Will's dysfunctional relationship with his best friend needs to come to its resolution. Tiny, sobbing, will express first his ignorance and then his pledge to be a better best friend, but first, Will must define friendship, which he does by listing the lengths to which he has gone to help Tiny: "You know what's important? Who would you die for? Who do you wake up at five forty-five in the morning for even though you don't even know why he needs you? Whose drunken nose would you pick?!"[25]

Clearing the air is all it takes, and the two boys are once again the closest friends—a successful strong relationship Erikson recognizes as a necessary accomplishment for moving on to adulthood.

Regardless of the nature of the desired relationship, rejection is always waiting in the wings to come on stage and spoil the show. In *An Abundance of Katherines*, girls "dumping" boys takes center stage, with Green disarming the hurt through humor, calculating the dumping incidents in an equation. In *The Fault in Our Stars*, Green appropriates adolescent humor again, through "preemptive dumping" and even "preempting the preemption."[26] Protagonists Hazel and Gus are on the verge of new love, but Hazel is having second thoughts in this conversation with her fellow cancer sufferer Kaitlyn:

> After a second, Kaitlyn said, "Remember Derek? He broke up with me last week because he decided there was something fundamentally incompatible about us deep down and that we'd only get hurt more if we played it out. He called it *preemptive dumping*. So maybe you have this premonition that there is something fundamentally incompatible and you're preempting the preemption."[27]

The humor doesn't stop there, however. Putting her own issues with Gus aside, Hazel expresses her condolences over Kaitlyn's lost love affair:

> "Sorry about Derek."
> "Oh, I got over it, darling. It took me a sleeve of Girl Scout Thin Mints and forty minutes to get over that boy."[28]

Readers may doubt that Kaitlyn so easily defused the hurt through chocolate, but they can't help but admire her attitude.

Unrequited love is one form of rejection, and so is death. Coping with death is hard at any age, but for adolescents, engaging with the reality of the death of a loved one can be a giant hurdle between childhood and adulthood. What can make it worse for young people is the feeling that they may be somehow complicit in someone's death. In *Looking for Alaska*, Pudge and the Colonel are trying to figure out if Alaska committed suicide or was just too drunk to drive and accidently crashed. Either way, they were guilty of failing to step in and prevent this tragedy. Not until the novel's end does Miles make a giant developmental leap forward, coping with Alaska's death in this way:

> When adults say, "Teenagers think they are invincible" with that sly smile on their faces, they don't know how right they are. We need never be hopeless, because we can never be irreparably broken. We think that we are invincible because we *are*. We cannot be born and we cannot die. Like all energy, we can only change shapes and sizes and manifestations. They forget that when they get old. They get scared of losing and failing. But that part of us greater than the sum of our parts cannot begin and cannot end, and so it cannot fail.
> So I know she [Alaska] forgives me, just as I forgive her.[29]

In addition to being beautifully poetic, these words express an idea that has been around for a long time, especially in the Bible. Genesis 3:19 says, "For dust you are and to dust you will return." Psalm 103:14 says, "[God] is mindful that we are but dust," and Psalm 78:39 says, "He remembered that they are but flesh, a passing breeze that does not return." Perhaps it is more accurately recalled as "carpe diem," used by the Roman poet Horace and meant as advice not to count on there being any tomorrow so make today count. It takes 136 days for Miles to come to the realization that he cannot hide from or in what he calls "the Labyrinth" of life but must continue to seek his way through the maze, continuing to believe in "the Great Perhaps," an allusion from François Rabelais.[30]

Like all adolescents, Miles empathizes with other teens who experience emotional pain, such as Lara, whom Green victimizes with both romantic rejection (dumping) and death. Miles imagines a hurt above all others when he sees his ex-girlfriend, who is also grieving over Alaska Young: "I wanted to talk to her. I knew I'd been awful— *Imagine*, I kept telling myself, *if you were Lara, with a dead friend and a silent ex-boyfriend.*"[31]

Intimacy can sometimes come with great emotional pain, the very penalty adolescents most dread, but the developmental need for close connections is mandatory.

Unfortunately, Erikson's "need for intimacy" stage is commonly accompanied by raging self-consciousness. And self-consciousness often turns to self-doubt or even self-loathing in the presence of members of the opposite sex. When Hazel first lays eyes on Gus in a cancer support group, her initial impulse is to obsess over imagined shortcomings:

> I looked away, suddenly conscious of my myriad insufficiencies. I was wearing old jeans, which had once been tight but now sagged in weird places, and a yellow T-shirt advertising a band I didn't even like anymore. Also my hair: I had this pageboy haircut, and I hadn't even bothered to, like, brush it. Furthermore, I had ridiculously fat chipmunked cheeks, a side effect of treatment. I looked like a normally proportioned person with a balloon for a head.[32]

Teenagers often create slang and new uses of language, including creative uses of conventions. According to Ani Khachatryan of Yerevan State University, invention of slang words can be "essential because [sometimes] there are no words in the standard language expressing exactly the same meaning,"[33] a fact not lost on Green. His characters are often inventive with language and its rules to suit their purpose. Will Grayson says, "Andbutso a week after we get back from Christmas break our junior year, I'm sitting in my Assigned Seat."[34] "Andbutso" actually serves pretty well as a sentence opener, and capitalizing "Assigned Seats" is surely a sarcastic attempt to make fun of the juvenile treatment kids receive in school.[35] Although it can't be done in spoken language, capitalization in written language serves well to express teen snarkiness, as when Will mocks his so-called friends in "I was busy having an actual honest-to-God Group of Friends for the first time in my life, who ended up Never Talking to Me Again."[36] When Gus in *The Fault in Our Stars* insists to Hazel that eggs have been unfairly cast as solely breakfast food, he invents the words he needs: "The thing about eggs, though," he said, "is that breakfastization gives scrambled eggs a certain *sacrality*, right?"[37] Neither "breakfastization" nor "sacrality" can be found in the Merriam-Webster or Cambridge dictionaries, but just as Lewis Carroll once had Humpty Dumpty proclaim, "When I use a word, it means just what I choose it to mean,"[38] readers know exactly what Gus means.

Another constant among Green's teens is pranking. At no age does the volume of practical joking rise to such a level as it does in adolescence. According to Benedict Carey of the *New York Times*, the best pranks are humorous coping mechanisms that do not rise to the level of being "dangerous or illegal,"[39] which surely fits Green's pranksters, whose shenanigans are usually harmless. The most common victim of adolescent pranks in Green's stories are authority figures such as parents or school officials, or peers who have proven themselves bullies and/or elitists.

The larger the prank and the more victims involved the better. In *Paper Towns*, Margo is known for pranks on a giant scale, such as toilet papering two hundred houses in one night, or breaking into Disneyland, acts she commits to get back at her parents. "Margo's parents suffer a severe narcissistic injury whenever she acts out," Quentin's therapist father explains, adding that he would probably behave similarly if he had such bad parents.[40] In *Looking for Alaska*, Alaska Young is determined that she and her friends, the poorer students at Culver Creek school, will pull the prank to end all pranks against the Eagle (Mr. Starnes, dean of students) and the Weekday Warriors, rich students who go home to luxury on the weekends. The prank involves leading the Eagle off on a wild-goose chase while they hack into the school computer and send bogus failing academic reports to the Weekday Warriors' parents and put blue dye in their shampoo. Creative revenge fulfills many of the developmental needs of adolescence—risk taking, challenging authority, and bonding with a peer group. Green's fictional pranks smack of the real deal.

And yet there is something innocent and sweet about Green's main characters. Will Grayson measures his level of sadness by the standard of how bad he felt at the end of *All Dogs Go to Heaven*. When he finds out Jane is at the botanical gardens for the day with an old boyfriend, he thinks, "I sure feel a hell of a lot worse than I did at the end of *All Dogs Go to Heaven*." Even when he wanders by mistake into a pornography shop at night in downtown Chicago, Will's thoughts and actions are endearing. He picks out a gay sex magazine for Tiny, *Mano a Mano*, explaining to a total stranger, "It's uh, for a friend," and then immediately thinks that he should have said, "I'm trying to learn Spanish."[41] Perhaps the sweetest of Green's characters is Gus in *The Fault in Our Stars*, who cares for his fellow cancer victim, Hazel, so much that he uses his wish from the Genies (a nonprofit that makes dying kids' dreams come true) to take Hazel to Holland, where he arranges a meeting with the author of her favorite book, *An Imperial Affliction*, so she can request answers providing closure to the book, which lacks a conventional ending.

Gus also provides hope, something all adolescents crave. In a yet unpublished study conducted in Phoenix, Arizona, adolescent readers were asked fifteen questions about the book they had found the most meaningful during the previous two years. The most common reason given for a choice was that the book had a teenager in a difficult situation, but no matter how bad the conditions were, the teen had hope. Although Hazel is actually the one closest to death throughout *The Fault in Our Stars*, a sudden relapse takes Gus's life before Hazel can catch her breath. At his funeral service, we discover what Gus provided to the other support group members—hope:

"Augustus Waters was the mayor of the Secret City of Cancervania, and he is not replaceable," Isaac began. "Other people will be able to tell you funny stories about Gus because he was a funny guy, but let me tell you a serious one: A day after I got my eye cut out, Gus showed up at the hospital. I was blind and heartbroken and didn't want to do anything, and Gus burst into my room and shouted, 'I have wonderful news!' And I was like, 'I don't really want to hear wonderful news right now,' and Gus said, 'This is wonderful news you want to hear,' and I asked him, 'Fine, what is it?' and he said, 'You are going to live a good and long life filled with great and terrible moments that you cannot even imagine yet!'"[42]

And that is the essence of the voice of John Green, resonating so strongly with adolescent readers: "You are going to live a good and long life filled with great and terrible moments that you cannot even imagine yet."

NOTES

1. John Green, home page, Nerdfighters, April 25, 2013, accessed January 12, 2015, http://nerdfighters.ning.com.

2. Stephen Roxburgh, "The Art of the Young Adult Novel," *ALAN Review* 32, no. 2 (2005): 7.

3. Northwest Regional Laboratory, "Trait Definitions," Education Northwest, accessed October 12, 2013, http://educationnorthwest.org/.

4. Marilyn Price-Mitchell, "What Happy Teens Do Differently," *Psychology Today*, July 15, 2013, accessed November 20, 2013, http://www.psychologytoday.com/.

5. John Green, *Will Grayson, Will Grayson* (New York: Dutton, 2010), 24.

6. John Green, *Looking for Alaska* (New York: Speak, 2005), 14.

7. Ibid., 13.

8. Ibid.

9. John Green, *An Abundance of Katherines* (New York: Dutton, 2006), 16.

10. Green, *Will Grayson*, 41.

11. John Green, *The Fault in Our Stars* (New York: Penguin, 2012), 16.

12. John Green, *Paper Towns* (New York: Dutton, 2008), 22.

13. Green, *Will Grayson*, 84.

14. Ibid.

15. Ibid., 85–86.

16. Green, *Looking for Alaska*, 140.

17. Lawrence Kohlberg, *Essays on Moral Development*, vol. 1: *The Philosophy of Moral Development* (San Francisco: Harper & Row, 1981).

18. Green, *Paper Towns*, 12.

19. Ibid., 14.

20. Green, *Fault in Our Stars*, 123.

21. Green, *Abundance of Katherines*, 131.

22. Erik Erikson, *Identity: Youth and Crisis* (New York: Norton, 1968).

23. "Erikson's Psychological Stages Summary Chart," About.com Psychology, last revised 2013, accessed November 9, 2013, http://psychology.about.com/.

24. Green, *Will Grayson*, 259.

25. Ibid.

26. Green, *Fault in Our Stars*, 95.

27. Ibid.

28. Ibid.

29. Green, *Looking for Alaska*, 220–21.

30. Ibid., 219.

31. Ibid., 189.

32. Green, *Fault in Our Stars*, 9.

33. Ani Khachatryan, "American Slang: The 20th Century," Academia.edu, accessed December 31, 2013, http://www.academia.edu/.

34. Green, *Will Grayson*, 6.

35. Ibid., 2.

36. Ibid., 3.

37. Green, *Fault in Our Stars*, 145.

38. Ibid., 72.

39. Benedict Carey, "April Fool! The Purpose of Pranks," *New York Times*, April 1, 2008, accessed October 2, 2013, http://www.nytimes.com/.

40. Green, *Paper Towns*, 106.

41. Green, *Will Grayson*, 108.

42. Green, *Fault in Our Stars*, 202.

Chapter Nine

Is John Green Really One of the One Hundred Most Influential People in the World?

John Green's influence in the world goes far beyond his award-winning books and their movie adaptations. In 2014, Green was named one of *Time* magazine's one hundred Most Influential People, a list that also includes US secretary of state John Kerry and even the US president himself, Barack Obama. According to Shailene Woodley's explanation of Green's place among the top one hundred, he is "more than just an author, artist, and innovator. I would go so far as to call him a prophet . . . in a universal, all-things-connected sort of context."[1] In addition to writing the Green tribute for *Time*, Woodley stars as Hazel Grace Lancaster, the protagonist in Temple Hill Entertainment's adaptation of Green's *Fault in Our Stars*. Woodley further explains that Green "treats every human he meets as their own planet, rather than simply one of his moons. He sees people with curiosity, compassion, grace and excitement. And he's encouraging a huge community of followers to do the same."[2]

And Green surely does some heavyweight encouraging. Consider his 2014 World Cup fundraiser, conducted to raise money for the Sarcoma Foundation of America by offering the opportunity for soccer enthusiasts to "vote for which team in the FIFA World Cup you want Hank and John to support by donating to the Sarcoma Foundation of

American through the Foundation to Decrease Worldsuck. 100% of donations will be given to SFA. One dollar, one vote."[3]

For this fundraiser, Green acquired athletic clothing for each of the thirty-two teams playing in the Fédération Internationale de Football Association (FIFA) World Cup, which enjoys the largest television audience of any sporting event in the world.[4] He could be seen wearing different jerseys and team T-shirts on his vlog announcing the fundraiser on May 27, 2014, as he explained that for every dollar donated by fans he would donate three dollars, 100 percent of which would go to the Sarcoma Foundation of America; he would wear the donor teams' jerseys or T-shirts on his vlog at some point;[5] and for each of the sixty-four matches he would cheer for the team that had the highest donations for the fundraiser.

As the World Cup came to an end, Green and his cohort had raised over $80,000 to fight sarcoma, a form of cancer that takes the life of Augustus Waters in Green's *Fault in Our Stars*. For donors who gave $10 or more, Green has provided a new short story, "The Space," which centers on a high school soccer player in West Virginia.[6]

The World Cup project to fight sarcoma was anything but a publicity stunt for the release of the *Fault in Our Stars* movie. Green's fundraisers for nonprofit charities have been going on for years, including his overarching annual Project for Awesome, which can be followed on YouTube at http://www.projectforawesome.com/. Project for Awesome annually contributes respectable amounts to respected causes in the world of philanthropy. Project for Awesome raised $869,171 in 2013 that went to a number of causes, such as a breast cancer victim-support fund, or a program for orphans in Zimbabwe.

Obviously, Green's connection to a worldwide community extends beyond the theater box office and Amazon.com. His major presence is online, where video blogs (vlogs) from Green and his brother Hank are nearly ubiquitous across the Nerdfighters ning, a variety of Facebook pages, and their Vlogbrothers YouTube channel, a channel with a subscribed membership of over 2,200,000. But thousands of authors have blogs, websites, and Facebook pages and all the usual cyber sustenance for their readers, so what makes Green's online presence different?

The answer to this question goes back to Shailene Woodley's observation that Green is "encouraging a huge community of followers to" engage their fellow human beings with "curiosity, compassion, and grace."[7] Green does not shy away from putting life into its proper moral perspective and urging his fans to step up to bat, a practice that is normally anathema to teens. His vlogs on how to lead a compassionate, honest, productive life, otherwise known by the Green brothers as fighting to "increase awesome and decrease suck," address the same topics that are often covered in the serious news, and not the fluff or pop culture topics more often reported in *Seventeen* or *Entertainment Tonight* or discussed on the typical fansites or author pages. Most author pages are primarily self-promotional, providing space for teen fans to share their love of the author's books, or donate to noncontroversial funds supporting victims of natural disasters such as hurricanes or earthquakes. Marketing wisdom holds it is best to be nonpolitical, noncontroversial, and keep a Teflon-like exterior to which no conflicting points of view may find a place to stick.

This is not the case for Green, who addresses new topics every week. Among the topics he has posted vlogs on are raising the minimum wage, the value of a college education, the national debt, binge drinking, dating, censorship, antifeminist aspects of the *Twilight* series, the crisis in Ukraine, health-care costs, and even how to become an adult. Youth heroes have typically avoided urging political and moral integrity, but Green is fearless in expounding on right and wrong. He is also adamant about thoughtfully examining all sides of each issue, as well as researching the context and background. Typically, he addresses either topics that are very close to the hearts of his teen audience members or controversial topics that are all over the news. In either case, he provides useful context and models logical thinking.

Some of these topics may seem remarkably equivalent to traditional adult recommendations of the "eat your vegetables," "don't do drugs," or "stay in school" type, such as Green's Vlogbrothers video "Is College Worth It?" In this video Green shows his work while doing the math to prove that the cost of college tuition and paying the interest on student loans is, in fact, more economically advantageous than forgoing a college education. But he doesn't stop there, and perhaps this is where Green's moral admonitions are different from the ones moms and dads give. Green goes deeper, down to the place where teens live, which is all about seeing past the adult obsession with financial or social status, down to what really counts: what will make my life worth living? Green explains that calculating the value of college based on dollars and cents alone misses the most important point:

> That calculation assumes that human life is a purely economic phenomenon. Which it isn't. . . . It has been my experience that maximizing

income is a helluva lot less important than maximizing passion and fulfillment both professionally and personally. . . . Whether you're studying electrical engineering or poetry, college is finally not about maximizing income; it's about becoming a better and more informed observer of the universe, and for me, at least, that's what leads to a more fulfilling life. In a world where about half of humans live on less than $2.50 a day, the opportunity to learn and study in a formal, dedicated way is still a gift, even if it has become a very expensive one.[8]

Green doesn't always walk his audience through a series of arithmetic calculations or logical progressions comparing various sides of an issue, however; sometimes he just clearly and passionately spells out his opinion. In the process, he may make assumptions about what intelligent people take for granted to be true without any argument needed. For example, in his video championing compulsory public education, "An Open Letter to Students Returning to School," he points out that for 99.9 percent of the history of the human race, a free, public education was not available to anyone. Yet now someone like NASA engineer Adam Steltzner can benefit from a free, public high school education and state-subsidized university bachelor's, master's, and doctoral degrees on the way to becoming the lead engineer on NASA's voyage to and exploration of Mars.[9] Green goes on to admit that school can be boring (as it was for him), but it provides us with an opportunity to do amazing things with our lives. More than that, it is of tremendous benefit to the human race:

Public Education does not exist for the benefit of students or the benefit of their parents. It exists for the benefit of the social order. We have discovered as a species that it is useful to have an educated population. You do not need to be a student or to have a child who is a student to benefit from public education. Every second of every day of your life, you benefit from public education.

So let me explain why I like to pay taxes for schools, even though I don't personally have a kid in school: It's because I don't like living in a country with a bunch of stupid people.[10]

On the Green brothers' Nerdfighteria wiki, a reposting of "An Open Letter to Public Education" had received nearly one million views, over seven thousand comments, twenty-five thousand likes, and only 310 dislikes as of July 2014.[11] This shorter and slightly revised version (above) appeared on Facebook on January 12, 2014. The message to young people is clear: education is crucial to the well-being of society, and you are lucky to be provided with free schools.

Topics like raising the minimum wage get so much play on cable television and print media that teens are likely to glaze over when the talking heads start pontificating on the social justice or the economic perils of raising the minimum wage.[12] Somewhere between MSNBC and Fox News lies the truth, and that truth may very well be John Green, who attempts to examine both sides before modeling how to arrive at an informed opinion. Green's vlog not only examines the issue but also teaches critical thinking. He asks the viewer to consider a hypothetical corndog fast-food restaurant, which he names Corndogs & Sodium, recognizing that at first glance it seems like having any required minimum wage to pay workers would hurt the business. He outlines the common argument that the free market will set the wages where they need to be because other fast-food restaurants in competition with Corndogs & Sodium are competing for workers, as well as competing for patrons. Offer too little pay and workers will choose to work for the restaurants that offer more, but pay your workers too much and you'll have to hire fewer. Since the cost of paying workers a higher wage will have to come from somewhere, you will either have to lower your profits (which could drive you out of business) or raise your prices (which could drive away your customers, and again, you're out of business). In order to stay in business yet pay a high enough wage to attract workers, you will arrive at a wage that keeps business going, thus illustrating the regulating effect of the free market at work.

Logical argument? It may seem so, and many people would stop there, but Green takes his young patrons onto a critical examination of this line of thinking:

> It turns out that actual labor markets are a lot more complex than the models created by college freshmen. This brings us to a famous study done by two economists, David Card and Alan Krueger. In 1992 the state of New Jersey raised its minimum wage by 18.8 percent. Pennsylvania, right next door, did not raise its minimum wage. Card and Krueger had the bright idea to go to the border of New Jersey and Pennsylvania and do employment surveys on either side of it. And what they found was that restaurant employment in New Jersey actually increased when the minimum wage went up. Since then a number of studies have confirmed Card and Krueger's findings although some other studies have found that there actually are negative effects to raising the minimum wage, but it's surprisingly and consistently mild.[13]

Green's bottom line seems to be that neither side of this argument has the corner on the truth, but moderately raising the minimum wage will have a mild, positive effect on the economy when done intermittently and sparingly. This variety of critical thinking and balanced consideration is rare in the news, but teens seem to be finding it refreshingly meaningful, hence the 670, 275 views of this vlog with a 97.5 percent thumbs-up rating on YouTube.

Censorship, on the other hand, is a controversy that affects young readers where they spend most of their day, in school. Green's books have been repeatedly challenged by groups opposing their use in public school curricula, including an incident in Depew, New York, in 2008. Two teachers at Depew High School proposed teaching *Looking for Alaska* to their eleventh-grade English-language-arts classes, and parents/guardians were given the option of signing a parent/guardian permission form if they approved. If parents/guardians did not sign the form, their child would read an alternative book already in the approved curriculum. According to Laura E. Winchester, reporting in the *Buffalo News*, two hundred people attended a school board meeting to discuss the use or misuse of the book at Depew High School.

> Super Tuesday had a different meaning at Tuesday's meeting of the Depew school board, which drew more than 200 people—primarily students—to address the unfolding controversy surrounding an award-winning novel that includes sexual material and graphic language.
>
> Attendance was fueled by book author John Green's YouTube video "I Am Not a Pornographer," in defense of his 2006 novel "Looking for Alaska," which has won numerous awards, including the Michael L. Printz Award for Excellence in Young Adult Literature. It also has been highly recommended by the American Library Association. [14]
>
> In the video, which has drawn more than 120,000 hits since its Jan. 30 posting, Green asked "nerdfighters" to attend Tuesday's meeting. He also suggested that those objecting to the book's material "should shut up and stop being condescending to teenagers." [15]

Winchester goes on to explain that five community members were given the floor to speak against the book, although no community members were given the floor to speak in favor of the book. According to Winchester, the National Council of Teachers of English provided the school district with a letter of support for Green's book, and Green himself sent a letter addressing the issue of alleged pornography as well. In lieu of the student majority in attendance, the reporter "spoke with nearly a dozen students before the meeting. All were in favor of the book and said the YouTube video had really sparked interest in the controversy."[16]

In the video "I Am Not a Pornographer," Green attempts to sort facts from false assumptions and to apply common sense to the situation, admittedly expressing what might be perceived as a biased opinion since he authored the book in question; however, he points out there are larger issues at hand here: parents' right to decide what their children can read in school, and what the book is really about, which is the opposite of what its detractors (none of whom had actually read the book) claimed:

[Community members who object to *Looking for Alaska*] think my book is pornographic and will cause immoral thoughts and actions in children, even those people whose parents signed the permission slip. These people believe that no one should be allowed to read the book. . . . I don't think there is a single halfway normal person in the world who would find a single thing in my book in anyway arousing. There is one very frank sex scene. It is awkward, un-fun, disastrous, and wholly unerotic. The whole reason that scene in question exists in *Looking for Alaska* is because I wanted to draw a contrast between that scene, when there's a lot of physical intimacy but it's ultimately very emotionally empty, and the scene that immediately follows it where there's not a serious physical interaction but there's this intense emotional connection. The argument here is that physical intimacy can never stand in for emotional closeness, and when teenagers conflate these ideas, it inevitably fails. It doesn't take a deeply critical understanding of literature to realize that *Looking for Alaska* is arguing against vapid physical interactions, not for them. Some people are going to say that kids don't have the critical sophistication when they're reading to understand that, and I have a message for those people: "Shut up and stop condescending to teenagers." Do you seriously think that teenagers aren't able to read critically? When they read George Orwell's *Animal Farm*, do they head to the pig farms to kill all the pigs because they're about to become communist autocrats? When they read *Huck Finn* do they think Huck should turn Jim in because the demented conscience of the community says so? When they read *Waiting for Godot*, do they think it's cool to just sit around and do nothing? Well, actually, probably they do; actually, that one doesn't really work toward my point. Now obviously, I don't think that few parents should get to decide what the kids of other parents read in school. Those parents are qualified to sign or not sign that permission slip as they see fit, and frankly, it pisses me off when small groups of well-organized book banners try to take over America's public school systems. Fortunately in Depew, there are a lot of teachers and school administrators and school board members who are standing up for my book, and for the right of teachers to teach it, and for the right of parents to choose to have it taught to their kids, but sometimes these people who make stands for intellectual freedom can feel like they're going it alone, which is why I would like to ask from the bottom of my heart that any nerdfighters who live in or around Depew go to the school board meeting on February 5, info in the sidebar. Also, I have written a letter in defense of the teachers who'd like to teach my book. If you'd like to write a letter, send it to sparksflyup@gmail.com, and I'll be sure to forward it on.[17]

What happened next after this video was released suggests an answer to the title of this chapter: "Is John Green Really One of the One Hundred Most Influential People in the World?" This video had over one million viewers on YouTube alone (it was also up on Facebook and on Green's website). Green's verbal appeal online to nerdfighters in the greater Buffalo, New York, area was heeded, and the majority of people attending the school board meeting that February 8, 2008, were in fact students. In the end, the six members of the Depew Union Free School District Board of Education voted unanimously to approve use of *Looking for Alaska*. In a time when young people may feel like powerless recipients of what society forces upon them, this was an incident of empowerment, and John Green was at the heart of it.

The world is a chaotic place, and in the last few decades, constant war has plagued the planet as one military coup replaces another, and national names and borders seem to change overnight. This is nothing new, but twenty-four-hours-a-day cable news networks provide a steady stream of disturbing images and news of further tragedies. No news provider is totally unbiased, and some news is unabashedly politically aligned, so who is a trusted source of interpretation? Edward R. Murrow provided that service to one generation; Walter Cronkite provided it for another, and Tom Brokaw for yet another. Perhaps John Green, even though he is not a journalist, is providing this trusted interpretation for young people today.

Green has no problem taking the time to provide historical background to current conflicts. In his Vlogbrothers video "Understanding Ukraine: The Problems Today and Some Historical Context," Green attempts to explain the military and political storm that has hit Ukraine for the last ten years, culminating in the annexation of Crimea by Russia in 2014. Green explains how the roots of this problem go back at least to the nineteenth century and include the deaths of more than two million people as various political and ethnic groups fought for control. Green attempts to provide three narratives for the current manifestation of the upheaval that has been going on for so long, one from the perspective of the ethnic Russians who live primarily in eastern Ukraine and in Crimea, one from the perspective of the Ukrainians who live in the western part of the country, and a third perspective that is Green's attempt at being objective:

> So here's one narrative of these events: An unpopular and ineffective but democratically elected politician was removed from power by a mob of protestors, and the new unelected parliament briefly passed a law that only Ukrainian can be the official language of the country, even though many people in the country speak Russian. Furthermore, this new government wants to become part of the EU, which might bring NATO missiles to Russia's border, and that is unacceptable to Russia. But here's another narrative: a tyrannical leader who ordered the murder of peaceful protestors was chased from power and replaced by a government that will transition Ukraine toward free and fair elections, and Russia responded to that by invading Ukraine. I'm trying to claim a false equivalence here, but I think it's important to understand both of these narratives, and I wanted to give a little more historical context than we've been seeing on the news because it helps us to understand that the pull between Western Europe and Russia in Ukraine is not new. I mean, the word "Ukraine" itself means "borderland." It has for centuries functioned as the border between West and East. What Ukraine needs is stability, decades of stability, so it can grow to have its own identity, to have relationships with both Europe and Russia without being controlled by either.[18]

Green goes on to explain that although that dream may seem impossible right now, historically this scenario has played out over and over in the world, eventually experiencing resolution in places like Japan, Germany, and Sierra Leone, all of which are experiencing peace and financial success currently.

The significance here is that, unlike most of the news and commentary young people hear through the media, Green attempts not to manipulate them but to give them the context and the plural perspectives they need to critically examine the issue of Crimea, Ukraine, and Russia's intervention. In history there are always multiple realities at play, a fact that American media often ignore. Green gives not the black-and-white Republican party line on Ukraine, nor the black-and-white Democratic party line on the country. He tries to tell the truth about a very complicated reality.

Generally, young adult fiction authors seem to be members of a mutual admiration society who never give anything less than rave reviews to their peers' work. Whether this is an unspoken truce for financial reasons or just professional courtesy, the practice of never emitting a single word of criticism seems somewhat disingenuous. Are no bad books for teens ever published, books that might be giving the wrong messages about life to young readers, maybe even harmful messages? For example, feminists have been quick to contend that the *Twilight* vampire series reproduces and reinforces some traditional cultural practices that are harmful to young women. Bella, the human protagonist, and Edward, her vampire love interest, may be a fantasy portrayal of the psychological dysfunction inherent in abusive relationships. *Psychology Today* columnist and Buena Vista University associate professor of psychology Dr. Wind Goodfriend points out how the "characteristics of Bella's relationship with Edward are actually templates for violence and abuse."[19] Goodfriend, a published expert on the characteristics of abusive romantic relationships, points to multiple unhealthy psychological elements in the series' relationship, exposing Edward for what he actually is, a manipulative stalker who robs his victim of her autonomy, and revealing Bella as the self-loathing, bad-boy-lusting people pleaser destined to find the man who will treat her as badly as her sick psyche demands. Goodfriend is only one of a large assembly of critics who say the book, which has proven to be candy to early teen girls, is starting them off on a path toward disaster.

Green agrees, and rather than jump on the *Twilight* bandwagon, he feels a sense of moral obligation to explain what's rotten in Forks, Washington. Respecting the intelligence of his reading audience, Green chooses not to lecture on the psychological perils of forbidden love. Instead, he fearlessly heralds the emperor's nakedness; *Twilight* is a story about a 107-year-old man who uses a seventeen-year-old body to seduce a sixteen-year-old girl (who never does put seventeen and ninety together and come up with the fact that she is dating her great-grandfather wearing a teenager mask). As Green puts it,

> This 107-year-old gets in a relationship with a 16-year-old girl, which for some reason isn't wrong. . . . I want to explain why it's wrong for adults to have romantic relationships with teenagers. It's not because we look old; it's because we ARE old. It's not a question of the youngness

and chiseledness of your pecs [picture of shirtless actor playing Edward in the movies]; it's a question of how many times you have been around the sun [Green gestures to indicate the passing of years]. Also in the *Twilight* books this girl Bella really needs dudes to take care of her because she is completely crazy without them, and you almost get the feeling from reading the book that a woman can't be whole until she has a strong, independent man in her life to take care of her, when of course the fact is that a woman needs a strong man to take care of her like a fish needs a bicycle. [20]

In concluding his vlog about *Twilight*, Green admits that he finds the books fun to read, the movies stupid, and the fantasy of idealized love at odds with the "criminality of 107-year-olds having romantic relationships with sixteen-year-old girls." He also recommends distinguishing between love and obsession.

Green's vlog on "How to Become an Adult" for people who are just about to finish school and join the adult workforce is not really about becoming an adult, although it starts off as a hilarious parody of such lectures:

One of the things you'll notice upon entering the "real world" is that it is neither more or less real than any of the previous worlds you have encountered. But you're likely to notice that the real world has this interesting mix of, like, crushing monotony and paralyzing terror. It's not a real world; it's more of a CMAPT world [crushing monotony and paralyzing terror]. Like there's the crushing monotony of waking up at the same time, sitting in the same traffic, going to the same job, and then coming home to pay the same bills, with your only distractions being like television and video games and YouTube. There's also the constant paralyzing terror of knowing that if you screw up sitting in traffic or working at your job or paying your rent, you will be, like, homeless, hungry, and alone. This is not to worry you or anything; this is just how it is for a lot of people. I will say that adulthood gets much, much better. Speaking of which, last night my son puked on my face, not on shirt or my shoulder or something, but on my actual sensory organs. [21]

Green goes on to explain that the big turning point in his adult life was meeting and enlisting the help of Ilene Cooper, American Library Association's *Booklist* children's books editor and successful author of more than thirty books for young readers. Green explains that Cooper helped him turn little more than an idea into the award-winning book

Looking for Alaska and that we all need to find a mentor to help us find our way.

In a complicated, constantly evolving world, what better mentor to help us find our way could we have than John Green?

NOTES

1. Shailene Woodley, "John Green: Author and Teen Whisperer," April 23, 2014, accessed June 10, 2014, http://time.com/.

2. Ibid.

3. "John Green: World Cup Fundraiser," Sarcoma Foundation of America: Finding the Cure in Our Time, May 27, 2014, accessed July 19, 2014, http://www.curesarcoma.org/.

4. "FIFA World CupTM Group Stages Break New Ground in TV Viewing," FIFA.com, June 28, 2014, accessed July 10, 2014, http://www.fifa.com/.

5. John Green, "All the Shirts (and Some Paths to Community)," Vlogbrothers, YouTube, May 27, 2014, accessed July 19, 2014, http://www.youtube.com/.

6. David Lindquist, "John Green Delivers New Story to Charity Supporters," *Indy-Star*, July 15, 2014, accessed July 17, 2014, http://www.indystar.com/.

7. Woodley, "John Green."

8. John Green, "Is College Worth It?" Vlogbrothers, YouTube, August 21, 2014, http://www.youtube.com/.

9. John Green, "An Open Letter to Students Returning to School," John Green, August 7, 2012, accessed July 1, 2014, http://johngreenbooks.com/.

10. Ibid.

11. John Green, "An Open Letter to Public Education," Nerdfighteria, accessed June 20, 2014, http://nerdfighteria.info/.

12. John Green, "Should We Raise the Minimum Wage?" Vlogbrothers, YouTube, February 4, 2014, accessed June 2, 2014, http://www.youtube.com/.

13. Ibid.

14. John Green, "I Am Not a Pornographer," Vlogbrothers, YouTube, January 30, 2008, accessed July 26, 2014, http://www.youtube.com/.

15. Laura E. Winchester, "Depew School Board Committee Will Review 'Coming-of-Age' Novel," *Buffalo News*, February 7, 2008.

16. Ibid.

17. Green, "I Am Not a Pornographer."

18. John Brown, "Understanding Ukraine: The Problems Today and Some Historical Context," Vlogbrothers , YouTube, March 4, 2014, accessed March 26, 2014, http://www.youtube.com/.

19. Wind Goodfriend, "A Psychologist at the Movies: Relationship Violence in 'Twilight,'" *Psychology Today*, November 9, 2011.

20. John Green, "John Reviews *Twilight* and *New Moon*," November 29, 2014, accessed June 19, 2014, http://www.youtube.com/.

21. John Green, "How to Become an Adult," Vlogbrothers, YouTube, August 31, 2011, accessed June 30, 2014, http://www.youtube.com/.

Chapter Ten

Before Alaska ... There Was Radio

The problem with much writing in schools is how false it is . . . they write in genres they have never read, or they read without attention to the work as situated in any particular discourse community other than the classroom.[1]

Readers develop a depth of knowledge through their understanding of an author's perspective. That understanding of how an author's life experiences influence his or her writing helps solidify the contractual relationship between author and reader: "Understanding how an author's life experiences influence his or her writing can assist readers with creating personal meaning and connections to the author's work."[2] This connection to an author's work is fostered through the reader's engagement with an author's dialogue; it provides another layer of insight and a more profound picture of the author.

Teachers, however, are often limited in their ability to expose students to anything other than the literature of authors they teach. Much of what is read in the schools is outdated and unrelated to the lives of today's young adults. Young adult (YA) authors have changed this, and not only are most of them *among* the living, but also their voices are ubiquitous. Readers can access blogs, Twitter, and Facebook pages; social media has connected readers with authors, and nowhere is this more prevalent than in the YA community. No longer are readers limited to sifting through complicated text to ascertain the hidden meaning or political agenda of the author. The Internet has opened a whole new world to the reader, one where he or she can access an author's perspective about real issues. John Green is an outstanding example of this transparency.

From 2002 to 2004, Green wrote and delivered a series of social commentaries on Chicago Public Radio. Like his novels, Green's commentary was born from his experiences. In these tirades, he is a young liberal who reads the world through a lens of humorous discontent—a persona not far removed from the characters in his novels. Like them, Green is a social and political misfit trying to function in an often-dysfunctional society.

2002, WBEZ CHICAGO

His first broadcast, airing on January 6, 2002, exposed the detriments of technology. Green admitted that his oscular history could be digitally reconstructed with the help of a Google search.[3] He was able, with a few keystrokes, to discover what became of his past girlfriends. Listeners were not only privy to a small slice of his romantic pursuits (nine to be exact) but also left to contemplate Green's recollection and subsequent classification of each encounter with nine ladies from his past. With this broadcast, Chicago Public Radio introduced a young aspiring author whose wit invited listeners to discussions about race, politics, and his own ever-evolving love life.

During his inaugural year on the radio, Green's commentaries ran the gamut. He spoke about relationships, politics, and equity at a time when listeners were still grappling with the effects of 9/11. Green dubbed Chicago "New York City's jealous little sister" and confronted the political idiocy that threatened the city's well-being. His broadcasting career began as a self-deprecation of his love life, or lack thereof, and progressed into a series of political and social challenges.

Green exposes himself as a "small-time American terrorist" upon discovering that his charitable contributions to the Global Relief Foundation were, unbeknownst to him, monetarily supporting a "morally questionable" cause. An effort, he surmised, for which he will never be punished because he is one of the *distinguishable* young, white citizens "who accidentally further the cause of terrorism."[4] The color of his skin prevents him from prosecution. Similarly, Green criticizes a federal government that seems to say, "When the constitution is inconvenient, ignore it," in response to the Jose Padilla case—in which the government chose to incarcerate an American citizen without charging him with a crime.[5] That same year, Green took on Chicago's parking laws, modestly proposing that the city rid itself of all vehicles by implementing a no-tolerance tow policy.[6] And days later, he challenged the state of Illinois' mandate that required gubernatorial candidates to be at least twenty-five years old—a mandate, according to Green, that perpetuates a deceptive pool of "young" and "fresh" politicians, none of whom were young and fresh. Green further established his brother, Hank, as a real potential "young" and "fresh" candidate, one who could not run for office because he was *too* young. Such laws, according to Green, are "idiotic" and "offensive"; they imply that the voters are not wise enough to determine the maturity of their candidates.[7] Evidently, Green's advocacy for the voice of youth was not solely relegated to his fiction.

As would be expected by current readers and nerdfighters, Green's treatise bared his less-than-stellar love life in 2002. Listeners would follow Green's journey, albeit a bumpy one, in search of true love. "The Game," also broadcast on January 6, 2002, revealed that Green lived in a walk-in closet, courtesy of his three roommates and compliments of his "former fiancée, who dumped [him] unceremoniously and left [him] to live a life of quiet desperation." His circumstance, however, was not without humor. Green wrote about "I Will," a game where the players barter a series of dares and the lowest bidder receives the honor of carrying out the dare. Green's dare, worth a whopping ten cents, was to propose to a complete stranger with the same ring with which he proposed to his *former* fiancée.[8] And so it goes.

His "Sparky" commentary, airing on September 26, 2002, tells the story of an Asian tree frog Green purchased with one of his former girlfriends. This frog was the proverbial "baby" that would save the relationship. It didn't. Consequently, Green was saddled with an amphibious "metaphor for failure and inadequacy," one that would urinate all over his tears. So, he set Sparky free in a local park, only to realize that his amphibious albatross could actually save Chicago from foreign ecological threats. Green's loss was Chicago's gain.[9]

In one of Green's final broadcasts, he mocked the practice of speed dating, a relatively new trend at the time. After embarking on over twenty dates in two hours time, "'dating' each mini-girlfriend for three minutes, he fell in love twice, feelings not reciprocated by either woman."[10] He closes his recitation of the experience quoting Gloria Gaynor's "I Will Survive," and we are left rallying for love's underdog.

2003, WBEZ CHICAGO

During his second year in radio, Green would tackle a strained economy, a controversial president in office, and an invasion that would put
America at war. While still maintaining a rather sarcastic radio persona,
he confronted political and economic tensions head on.

His initial broadcast, airing on January 6, 2003, brazenly attacked
corporate greed. United Airlines, on the verge of bankruptcy, asked the
government for a two-billion-dollar loan. This loan was in addition to
the initial billion-dollar bailout already administered to the airline in-
dustry and a direct response to the fact that the airline was losing
approximately nine million dollars a day. Green advised the airline of
his own three-tiered plan to foil the creditors. He quipped, "John Green
Incorporated could afford to lose nine million dollars a day for about
seven seconds," acknowledging why it was so difficult for anyone to
feel bad for greedy corporations. [11] He was quick to admonish capitalis-
tic ideology and began to speak up for his own twentysomething generation, a generation that would soon see its country go to war.

The United States invaded Iraq on March 13, 2003. For many, this
invasion was inevitable. Green grappled with war, an idea that his
generation had only known through television shows and history
books. His broadcast on February 10, 2003, aptly titled "Like, A War,"
asked his listeners to consider, "If the United States pursues its new-
found policy of preemptively striking regimes it believes may one day
pose a threat to our national security, the men and women of my generation will learn the true meaning of war soon enough—and I suspect it
won't be nearly as comical as they made it out to be on M*A*S*H." [12]

The conflict fueled much of Green's subsequent discourse in 2003.
In "Let Us Now Praise Famous Bushes," he introduces Katherine, a
Republican former girlfriend—as unbelievable as it seems—and her
belief that the misfortune of poor people was a direct result of their lack
of intelligence. This lack of empathy for the less fortunate, according to
Green, was a relatively common perception of anyone in the Republican Party. He begins to realize, however, that the Republican Party, as
a whole, was not like his ex-girlfriend but rather more like himself:
"passionate, idealistic, and utterly irresponsible." [13]

Six days after the United States invaded Iraq, Green explores his
"deep-seated protest-related anxieties." Admittedly not much for protesting, he voices his opposition toward the war. [14] This outspoken,
unpopular, radical, albeit honest, discourse attracted listeners to his

broadcasts and would eventually draw readers to his young adult characters; they care about their world despite their inability to comprehend it.

Green's expositions during spring and early summer of 2003 maintained his sardonic tone towards injustice. He continued to champion free speech and the less fortunate, but his commentary shifted to his personal life. After suffering a ridiculous rent raise, Green shared his "Five Simple Rules for Moving," an economic advice column for displaced renters. This broadcast, while still denigrating the control of wealth, admonished the mover who hated moving. Green simplifies the process of moving because "there's nothing that puts a chill down the spine of Chicago real estate barons like a renting populace unafraid of taking a hike."[15] After all, nothing is more frightening to the bully than a populace that refuses to be bullied.

During the latter part of 2003, Green expressed his sentiments on the new Soldier Field, where tailgating space—the crucial pregame celebratory space for die-hard sports fans—was sacrificed for more parking spaces.[16] He recounted the tale of a reckless and dangerous bike messenger who broke his nose in a collision.[17] He paid tribute to yet another move.[18] And he pled with the Chicago Cubs for a World Series appearance . . . someday.[19] But Green's final broadcast, titled "On Winter," really captured the hope and promise of his personal and professional life. In what can only be described as a pep talk to himself, Green identified Chicago as a "cold" city—both literally and metaphorically—and while not asking her to cease being her "frigid self," he sought middle ground. We are left to wonder if 2004 will bring him promise rather than abandonment. Perhaps Chicago wasn't as welcoming as his hometown of Orlando, Florida, nor did he feel welcome in his brief tenure in Pelham, Alabama. Winter—"liquid nitrogen . . . chilling the depths of your human soul"—forces Green to question whether he can take the upper hand with his "irredeemably cold town."[20] After all, it has delivered little but corrupt politicians, failed relationships, and disappointing sports teams. He eventually chastises himself to "stop compromising . . . every ethical principle in hopes that you won't be abandoned by cities and girls and friends and jobs and the rest of it." It appears to the listener that promise is on the horizon and Green has reconciled himself with Chicago. The year 2004 looms as a year of possibility.

2004, WBEZ CHICAGO

As he did in previous years, in 2004 Green discussed a wide spectrum of issues. Again, he interspersed tales of his love life with his social and political commentary. And with good reason: 2004 was the year that Green met Sarah, his future wife.

Green satirized Jack Ryan, a Republican candidate for Senate, who was forced to vacate his seat because of scandalous allegations that he frequented sex clubs with his ex-wife. In his letter of application putting himself forward as a candidate for Ryan's seat, Green admitted that his qualifications were lacking. First, he was not a Republican. Second, he was too young for the job (candidates had to be at least thirty years old). Yet, he pled for consideration because he was the "profoundly honest man" needed by voters in Chicago in order to "regain faith in the Republican Party." Green further prophesized the inevitability of a Republican loss, something that also made him appealing as a candidate: "You'll be hard-pressed to locate a finer loser than me."[21]

Green's broadcast on February 26, 2004, entitled "Sex Mathematics," demanded all of the kisses he had apparently been denied by the city of Chicago. His sexless life had left him almost sixty-eight thousand (67,996 to be exact) kisses short of what his calculations had determined was owed to him—a debt that appeared to be paid in full by year's end.[22]

Prior to revealing his relationship on radio, however, Green advocated the banning of school in response to a school in Merrillville, Indiana, that banned the color "pink" because it was affiliated with a local gang.[23] He vocalized his disappointment with his Chicago Bears, who had contracted with Bank One for sponsorship.[24] He questioned the issue of Mayor Daley's installation of surveillance cameras throughout the city of Chicago.[25] He explored the issue of credit cards at fast-food restaurants.[26] And he shared his very personal account of his own health scare that warranted a colonoscopy.[27] But it is his broadcast on November 26, 2004, that revealed the upswing in his personal life: "I am staying on the sinking ship of Chicago, and I'll tell you why. My girlfriend."[28] He will go down with this ship called Chicago. His listeners couldn't have been happier. Green's girlfriend (now his wife) was mentioned a couple more times in 2004. But his last post hints at the publication of his first novel, "Uncle Tom," titled for his great uncle, John Thomas Goodrich, and offers insight into John's vocation as a writer. Uncle Tom published his first novel in 1932 when he was twenty-seven. Green reveals that *his* first novel will be published in 2005, when he too is twenty-seven. And, like his uncle, he has a deep affection for booze and Los Angeles.[29] The first is a testament to the curse of many writers; the latter is a tribute to the place where he met Sarah (the Yeti).

So while 2003 closed with promise, 2004 delivered it. Green's final broadcasts, three of which aired in 2005, still tackled political and social issues and maintained his witty repertoire of insults and questions. But it was the publication of his first novel that really gained him the adoration of young adults.

> I like publishing the way I publish partly because it reminds me that books are supposed to do something other than just prove to the reader that the author is intelligent. . . . I'm very prone to that kind of self-indulgence, and honestly it is only when I am writing for teenagers that I feel like I am doing work that is *useful.*
> —John Green[30]

Looking for Alaska introduced young adults to an author whose social commentary, primarily written and broadcast for an adult audience, further characterized the unsung heroes in each of his novels.

> I mean, to be totally honest with you, I don't really give a shit about adults.
> —John Green[31]

NOTES

1. Anne Elrod Whitney, Michael Ridgeman, and Gary Masquelier, "Beyond 'Is This Okay?' High School Writers Building Understandings of Genre," *Journal of Adolescent and Adult Literacy* 54, no. 7 (April 2011): 525.
2. Denise Johnson, "Teaching with Authors' Blogs: Connections, Collaboration, Creativity," *Journal of Adolescent and Adult Literacy* 54, no. 3 (February 2010): 176.
3. John Green, "Nine Girls I've Kissed and What I Learned About Them from Google," John Green, January 6, 2002, accessed January 14, 2015, http://johngreenbooks.com/.
4. John Green, "The Accidental Terrorist," John Green, February 26, 2002, accessed January 14, 2015, http://johngreenbooks.com/.
5. John Green, "Illinois' Budget Fixed by al-Qaeda Operative," John Green, February 26, 2002, accessed January 14, 2015, http://johngreenbooks.com/.
6. John Green, "A Modest Proposal," John Green, October 5, 2002, accessed January 14, 2015, http://johngreenbooks.com/.

7. John Green, "Your Next Governor," John Green, October 21, 2002, accessed January 14, 2015, http://johngreenbooks.com/.

8. John Green, "The Game," John Green, January 6, 2002, accessed January 14, 2015, http://johngreenbooks.com/.

9. John Green, "Sparky," John Green, September 26, 2002, accessed January 14, 2015, http://johngreenbooks.com/.

10. John Green, "Speed Dating," John Green, November 26, 2002, accessed January 14, 2015, http://johngreenbooks.com/.

11. John Green, "Flying High on Corporate Welfare," John Green, January 6, 2003, accessed January 14, 2015, http://johngreenbooks.com/.

12. John Green, "Like, A War," John Green, February 10, 2003, accessed January 14, 2015, http://johngreenbooks.com/.

13. John Green, "Let Us Now Praise Famous Bushes," John Green, March 6, 2003, accessed January 14, 2015, http://johngreenbooks.com/.

14. John Green, "The Unbearable Lightness of Protesting," John Green, March 18, 2003, accessed January 14, 2015, http://johngreenbooks.com/.

15. John Green, "Five Simple Rules for Moving," John Green, June 26, 2003, accessed January 14, 2015, http://johngreenbooks.com/.

16. John Green, "The New Soldier Field," John Green, June 26, 2003, accessed January 14, 2015, http://johngreenbooks.com/.

17. John Green, "The Last Time I Broke My Nose," John Green, June 26, 2003, accessed January 14, 2015, http://johngreenbooks.com/.

18. John Green, "Moving (Again)," John Green, September 26, 2003, accessed January 14, 2015, http://johngreenbooks.com/.

19. John Green, "Kissing the Cubs," John Green, October 26, 2003, accessed January 14, 2015, http://johngreenbooks.com/.

20. John Green, "On Winter," John Green, December 26, 2003, accessed January 14, 2015, http://johngreenbooks.com/.

21. John Green, "John Green for Senate," John Green, January 12, 2004, accessed January 14, 2015, http://johngreenbooks.com/.

22. John Green, "Sex Mathematics," John Green, February 26, 2004, accessed January 14, 2015, http://johngreenbooks.com/.

23. John Green, "Pink, as Heard on WBEZ," John Green, April 26, 2004, accessed January 14, 2015, http://johngreenbooks.com/.

24. John Green, "Da Bankones," John Green, May 26, 2004, accessed January 14, 2015, http://johngreenbooks.com/.

25. John Green, "Surveillance," John Green, July 28, 2004, accessed January 14, 2015, http://johngreenbooks.com/.

26. John Green, "Faster Is Better," John Green, September 5, 2004, accessed January 14, 2015, http://johngreenbooks.com/.

27. John Green, "The Colonoscopy," John Green, October 25, 2004, accessed January 14, 2015, http://johngreenbooks.com/.

28. John Green, "Fattening Up and Rising Down," John Green, November 26, 2004, accessed January 14, 2015, http://johngreenbooks.com/.

29. John Green, "Uncle Tom," John Green, December 17, 2004, accessed January 14, 2015, http://johngreenbooks.com/.

30. John Green, John Green's Tumblr, http://fishingboatproceeds.tumblr.com/.

31. Ibid.

Chapter Eleven

Crossing Over

Young adult literature has matured into something virtually indistin-
guishable from the best adult literary fiction.
—Jonathan Hunt

In September 2012, *Publishers Weekly* claimed that 55 percent of
young adult (YA) books were bought by adults, eighteen years or older.
In fact, the largest segment of consumers, accounting for 28 percent of
total sales, were readers aged thirty to forty-four.[1] And 78 percent of
those adults admitted to purchasing YA books for their own reading.
Today's adult reader, it appears, is less likely to fall prey to the elitism
that permeates literature.

This literary phenomenon is often referred to as crossover, or books
that are published for one audience (in this case, young adults) but also
have appeal for another category of readers. While teens were once
encouraged to graduate to a more sophisticated, more adult body of
literature, today it appears the opposite rings true. More adults are
reading young adult books than ever before.

But what is it that characterizes a book as young adult? Jonathan
Stevens, in an attempt to define the genre, explains, "'Young Adult'
refers to a story that tackles the difficult, and oftentimes adult, issues
that arise during an adolescent's journey toward identity, a journey told
through a distinctly teen voice that holds the same potential for literary
value as its 'Grownup' peers."[2]

The young adult novel is written about teens and typically told in
the first person, elements that often stigmatize the genre. This journey

toward identity, however, adds to rather than detracts from a book's literary value. Prototype adolescent protagonists—Tom Sawyer, Huck Finn, Pip, and Holden, to name a few—navigated through the experimental forms created by their respective authors. Each young character became lost in a world that failed to value him, one where his moral integrity often surpassed that of his adult counterparts. And yet, several critics continue to question the value of young adult literature because young adult protagonists are created with the adolescent reader in mind.

The modern crossover novel, however, beckons the discriminating young adult reader; it "requires more serious concentration from young readers and helps move them from the pleasures of light reading to the pleasures of literary reading," while it satisfies the adult literary palate.[3] While this phenomenon is not necessarily surprising to young adult authors or advocates, many of whom have argued the literary merits of the genre for some time, it can be polarizing. Maggie Stiefvater, author of *Shiver, Linger, The Raven Boys,* and several other young adult novels, argues that labeling books as either "adult" or "young adult" privileges one audience over the other:

> As gatekeepers—and every adult in any segment of the book business, from author to librarian to teacher to bookseller is a gatekeeper—we have to give teens the credit they deserve. They are young adults. ADULTS. That means that they are as varied in their reading tastes and abilities as adults are. They don't need watered down versions of adult books—unless you acknowledge that there are adults, too, that also need watered down versions of those books.[4]

Young adult readers are independent thinkers with discriminating tastes. Strong young adult authors—often viewed as reputable crossover authors—according to librarian and critic Jonathan Hunt, "make no concessions and no compromises." John Green is one of those authors. His young adult novels have crossover appeal, not only because he tells a good story, but also because he values the literary sophistication of the young adult reader. When asked whether he felt he needed to defend his choice to write for the young adult reader, Green replied, "In the long run, the whole genre debate doesn't matter. Your books will stay around or they won't."[5] Based upon the overwhelmingly positive response from adults and young adults, Green's books are destined to stay around.

REDISCOVERING THE FOUNTAIN OF YOUTH

Adults who aren't teachers or parents miss a great deal by walking past the shelves labeled young adult literature in libraries and bookstores. . . . [We must] dispel the myth that YA literature is lightweight. Until adult readers can convince the reading public that these are everybody's books, we'll continue to be secret sharers of literature that not only encourages us to remember, but reminds us how important it is not to forget.[6]

Young adults have long been "secret sharers" of literature. They are tenacious readers, discriminating readers, and loyal readers. Plot lines must be plausible, and characters must be believable. In essence, what comprises good young adult literature is the same thing that comprises good adult literature. Adults are paying attention to young adult literature, something worthy of further study.

Initially, this chapter was created with a vision of presenting a slice of teen perspective on John Green and his books. In response to the recent firestorm surrounding not only his books but also his universal appeal to both young adults and adults, we decided to present the multiple perspectives, albeit only a sampling, of both adolescents and adults. Age, in this case, is simply a number.

THE YOUNG ADULTS

Madison: At the time of the interview, Maddie was fourteen and in ninth grade. She enjoys reading, running cross-country, and performing in school musicals.

Skylar: At the time of the interview, Skylar was fifteen and in ninth grade. She enjoys running, cross-country, reading, and playing the piano.

Kim: At the time of the interview, Kim was sixteen years old and a junior in high school. She enjoys reading, playing soccer, playing basketball, and performing in school musicals.

THE YOUNG ADULTS AT HEART

Jenn: Four days prior to the interview, Jenn celebrated her thirtieth birthday. She is a preservice English teacher enrolled at Metropolitan State University of Denver. She will complete her student teaching in spring 2015.

Liz: Liz is twenty-five, a preservice English teacher enrolled in her final semester of coursework at Metropolitan State University of Denver. She will complete her student teaching in spring 2015.

Bobby: Bobby is a fifty-year-old English teacher, enrolled in a post-baccalaureate English program at Metropolitan State University of Denver. He teaches twelfth grade at a school in Denver.

Amy: Amy is a licensed clinical psychologist. She is seventy years old and discovered John Green's book *The Fault in Our Stars* five months prior to the writing of this chapter.

IN THEIR WORDS

How do you see yourself as a reader? Have you always liked to read? Do you read regularly inside/outside of school or work?

Madison: Actually, I haven't always liked to read. When I was younger, in elementary school, I didn't like to read that much, but at the end of middle school going into high school I started reading a lot more. I like some of the books I read in school—not all of them—but I like reading a lot on my own. [7]

Skylar: I'd say I'm a pretty avid reader. I always keep track of the books I read because I like to know, so last year I read sixty books, and this year I'm trying to set a goal of seventy-five, so I read a lot more outside of school. In school, we read some books, and I usually enjoy them, but I enjoy reading outside of school much more than in school. [8]

Kim: I haven't always liked to read. I would say that I'm not a big reader, but when I find something that I do like to read, I will read it. [9]

Liz: As a reader I think I've always been very avid. I started at a young age. My parents were giving me books all the time. And I still continue to read inside and outside of school. I really enjoy reading YA books. [10]

Jenn: I read a lot. I love to read, but I didn't always love to read. I come from a family of incredibly strong readers—my mom has read books while I was taking a nap. My parents once ran out of bookshelf space, and they put books on top of the kitchen cabinets to make book space. The kitchen cabinets broke under the

weight of the books. In comparison, I'm dyslexic. I grew up
thinking reading was like breathing: an easy and enjoyable thing
to do. But it wasn't for me. I consistently tried to read; I really
struggled with it. Mostly because I had this idea of what it
should be and it wasn't for me.[11]

Bobby: I have not always read. I am dyslexic, and I struggled in
elementary school and high school. In middle school, I got
turned on by *The Outsiders*. A teacher helped me read by encouraging me to read and listen to music at the same time, and
that helped me out a lot. Now I read a lot more. I usually have a
book going all the time. I still struggle; it probably takes me a
good fifteen to twenty minutes to get into a good rhythm when
I'm reading. I read mostly YA lit.[12]

Amy: I am an avid reader; it is my "addiction." [I have been read-
ing] since age four . . . every night before I go to bed and every
chance I get. I do not watch TV and spend the time reading that
others would spend watching TV.[13]

When and how did you first become acquainted with John Green's books?

Madison: Seventh or eighth grade. And it was actually Skylar who
said, "Oh my gosh! I loved the book *The Fault in Our Stars*,"
and I'm like, okay, I'll read it. And now I've read it about *six*
times. I have read *The Fault in Our Stars, Looking for Alaska*,
and *Paper Towns*. And soon I will be reading *An Abundance of
Katherines*.

Skylar: I watched John Green's videos on YouTube. He collabo-
rates with his brother on Vlogbrothers, and I found him to be
really intelligent and inspiring. So, I picked up *The Fault in Our
Stars* because he had just released it. . . . I read it and it was
amazing! So, I read all of his other books too.

Kim: I enjoyed reading the Harry Potter series and then Skylar
showed Madison the John Green books and Madison showed me
The Fault in Our Stars, and it kind of . . . I liked that genre, I
guess. It's about the *only* type of book I like to read, honestly.
I've [also] read *The Fault in Our Stars, Looking for Alaska*, and
Paper Towns.

And now let's hear from the adults:

> Why is adult response important? Because one of the loudest criticisms
> of young adult literature is that its appeal is limited. . . . It's no secret
> that many adults, even teachers, are condescending in their views of
> young adult literature. . . . Such condescension reveals a failure to keep
> abreast of the latest developments in literature. [14]

Liz: In my young adult literature class, spring 2012, we read *Looking for Alaska* and *Fault in Our Stars*. I didn't know YA was
really a genre, so that class really opened my eyes to a bunch of
stuff.

Jenn: I had heard a little bit about him, but the first time I had read
his books was in my young adult literature class in summer
2013. I read FIOS and then proceeded to read all his other novels.

Bobby: I took a YA lit course. I read *Looking for Alaska* in that
class, and I just recently read *The Fault in Our Stars*.

Amy: A good friend whose taste is similar recommended *The Fault
in Our Stars*.

As a reader, what specifically makes you such a fan of John Green's books?

> Schools have failed to recognize the value of young adult literature. . . .
> Ignorance of the power this literature has to evoke in students the kind
> of literary experience that will keep them reading and lead them to a
> deeper understanding of literature in general, and the relationship be-
> tween literature and life in particular. [15]

Madison: I don't know . . . I just like them because of how it's about
teenagers and different things they go through, like the cancer
thing in *The Fault in Our Stars*. I just like the different stories.

Skylar: I think his books are really real. There's an element that you
don't get from other authors that displays a quality of real life,
and they're honest and I find the characters to be intelligent and
witty but still kind and relatable at the same time. They don't
have some superhero aspect to them, and they're very relatable
to me.

Kim: I like the way he keeps you interested. There's never really a
boring part in the book. It's very relatable topics—like being an

outcast or not fitting in places. He writes about that, and that happens a lot nowadays in high school and stuff like that, so it relates. It's cool.

I'll never forget the first time I read a book that awoke my emotions. I was alone in a hotel room, on a college basketball road trip. As I turned the last page of the novel, I found myself on the verge of tears. The feeling was so foreign, I felt guilty. Soft.
—Matt de la Peña[16]

Liz: He's got a lot of emotion and passion in his writing. He kept me engaged, which is something that I really appreciated. I lose interest really quickly, and his books make me *want* to keep reading.

Jenn: The way that he portrays teenagers is honest. I would read his books and remember having those feelings. I love the snarky way that he portrays teenagers: their wit and their intelligence while also tackling the issues that teenagers face.

Bobby: His use of language and [his] accessibility. The characters are very accessible to me, and I gravitate to them. There is always something that I can relate to whether male or female, something about his characters that is very endearing to me.

Amy: I thought it was very well written, extremely sensitive, and the topic was different, although painful, and excellent.

What is your favorite John Green book and why?

The growing depth and breadth of young adult literature cannot come at a better time. Today's American teenagers are one of the most diverse generations ever. They want and need literature that affirms who they are and offers insight into their world.
—Beth Yoke[17]

Madison: *The Fault in Our Stars.* I love Augustus Waters and the romance between them and the teenagers and love.

Skylar: I really like *Looking for Alaska.* That's my favorite. I think Pudge's character and the search for the great perhaps kind of . . . I don't know; I always thought that if you looked for something better in life, you'd be happier. I think how he learns to deal with death and how he tries to find answers even after she's gone, I think that's really interesting and something you can relate to easily: the search for something more after someone's gone—after they die or after they leave. I think the characters are really developed and strong throughout the entire novel.

Kim: I like *The Fault in Our Stars* and *Paper Towns* the best. I like in *Paper Towns* how this kid is kind of a misfit and in a band group and he's in love with this girl who's popular and then they become friends and it's just the adventure that he goes through. He goes the distance to try to find her again—what he does for her even though he doesn't technically really know her that well. And in *The Fault in Our Stars*, it's just the story of her having cancer and him having cancer and what they have to deal with and how they go through life together and how they deal with day-to-day life.

Liz: *Looking for Alaska*. The plot line was something that I had never experienced, and I couldn't see what was happening. Again, when I see where a story is going I lose interest and his books keep me guessing.

Jenn: Probably *The Fault in Our Stars*; it was the first of his books that I had read. I found myself reading quotes out loud. It was engaging to me, not just another book about teenagers with cancer.

Bobby: For right now, *The Fault in Our Stars* because it's freshest in my mind. I really loved his language in that book. I liked his connection to Shakespeare, I liked the theme. In hindsight, *Looking for Alaska* was a little more adventurous. More risk taking.

Amy: The only book of his I have read to date is *The Fault in Our Stars*, although I want to read more of them.

Why are so many adults reading young adult books? No need to page Dr. Freud. This isn't about the guilty pleasures of communing with one's inner child. It doesn't signify a huge baby boomer regression. It isn't even about nostalgia.

It's because adults are discovering one of publishing's best-kept secrets: that young adult authors are doing some of the most daring work out there.

—Patricia McCormick[18]

How would you respond to those who believe that some of John Green's books should be banned in schools because of inappropriate content?

Next time you want to get a book for your thirteen-year-old, send her . . . with a few bucks to buy what she wants. Take a look at it. Read it with her. Talk about what you like and don't like, and *learn* what *she* likes and doesn't like . . . the freedom to read includes the freedom not to read. Put yourself into that enviable spot of being someone to turn to when your daughter's life, from her point of view, matches up with some book, because as much as you think—or hope—it won't, trust me, it will. When it does, if she thinks she will be diminished in your eyes, she'll go elsewhere for help.

—Chris Crutcher[19]

Madison: I remember there was some sexual stuff, some smoking, and that they did drink, but I don't remember specifically what or when in the book they did that. I got a lot of enjoyment out of the books; a lot of tears came out of the books. I was very sad, kind of depressed actually. They were just good books and were fun to read, and some parts were hilarious and others were sad, and they were just enjoyable books that were fun to read for me.

Skylar: I've actually heard a lot about this, especially with *Looking for Alaska*, because . . . John Green talked about it. I think actually, I think it's pretty ridiculous to ban them. The books themselves—they don't promote that stuff throughout most of the book. It shows the corruptness of it. Like Alaska, she smokes and stuff, and she even says that she doesn't do it for fun. She does it because she's so sad and stuff. And I think kids should be exposed to this and then they learn how to deal with it. If we keep it all inside and keep it hush hush, then kids look for it and look to explore it. I think reading books has helped me realize there are very bad prospects of doing those things. I'd encourage the parent, if they're really worried, [to] read with their child, because if not, they're going to find a way to read the book by themselves and they'll get their questions answered by someone else. It would be better if [advice] came from [parents] than from another source. I definitely encourage [parents] to read with their children.

Kim: I don't feel like it's going to corrupt them (youth) because it's in the society. It's not like they haven't heard about it. It's not like kids aren't hearing about people smoking and drinking; that's happening. And writing about it is just going to . . . I don't feel like it's really going to do much. I don't think it's going to encourage people. They should know that what's bad is bad. Kids *do* do it; our age, that happens . . . it's out there and people advertise it . . . it's in the community—people know about it— and banning books just makes kids want to read them more . . . so I feel like there's no point in banning something because kids are going to want to read it anyway. I definitely agree with Skylar that the parent may be able to offer their own input while they're reading it with their child and tell them, well, this is what could happen if you were to smoke at that age, and they could know what their child is thinking when reading the book and maybe clear things up and explain things better than a teacher would be able to do in a classroom setting.

Jenn: I think that this has been going on for so long. Teenagers are going to read these books regardless, if you think that these books are too adult for them, you are not in touch with what's going on with teenagers.

Bobby: I'm not a fan of banning any books. Freedom of expression, read what you want. Parents should guide their children, but don't ban books.

Amy: I do not believe that young readers can be corrupted by what they read especially if there is someone who can help them understand the information. I believe you expose children to different thoughts and ideas to help them understand life.

If you had the opportunity to speak to John Green about his books, what would you want him to know?

When I visit schools, the students tell me about books they "have to read." Their recommendations are almost always young adult titles. Not because that category is necessarily better than the canon, but because they identify with the characters, because they're living the stories. And some of today's most exciting authors are writing young adult fiction. I believe many of tomorrow's canon can be found in today's young adult section.

—Matt de la Peña[20]

Madison: I'd want him to know that if he's going to write another book, could someone please not die for once? He is an amazing author and my favorite author.

Skylar: Thank you. Before I read his books, I read books, but I didn't think about what I was reading or think about what other things I could be reading too. His books really opened me up to a different community, I would say, of readers and authors that I could relate to—another place I could escape to when school or my family is hard, that I know is always there for me. I follow his video updates, as soon as he releases a video. I wouldn't say I'm really involved in the community, but he does a lot of charity work, like Project for Awesome every year when he donates money, and I always try to donate money or do anything that can help out with that community because I think that it's a really great, strong one (project).

Kim: I'd tell him he's very good at writing about day-to-day life, [about] what real problems happen to adolescent[s]. Just the way that he puts things and the way that he explains . . . life and tragedies that happen and . . . experiences kids have to go through that they shouldn't have to . . . he does that very well.

Liz: From a teaching standpoint I think his books have made a huge impact on me. His books really relate to kids. Kids are struggling with internal and external pressures like his characters . . . he writes books for those kids.

Jenn: I'm sure that he does, but just to make him aware of how universal the love of his books really is. I've read them for YA lit classes so that I can be more aware of what my students will be reading. And then I turned around and gave the same books to my mother and my brother for Christmas, both of whom are adults, because they are the kind of books that were written for everybody. For somebody who really struggled as a reader, I have these moments where I will be wearing my *Fault in Our Stars* backpack or sunglasses and adults will stop me and strike up a conversation. I now can discuss reading with people, something I wasn't able to do when I was younger. It has become a part of my larger life. His whole idea of Nerdfighters and DFTBA [don't forget to be awesome] is something that is engaging people on so many levels. That's an amazing thing to come from books; he has created an amazing culture.

Bobby: His books are at the top of my list as far as referring to kids who are not dedicated readers. It gives them an avenue into reading; they can take their time with it. The characters and the story lines are so believable and there is so much substance that the students whom I work with—the nonreaders—will continue to read. His books have similar effects on my students as *The Outsiders* had on me. Most of my students have some sort of label—dyslexia, ADHD, some end of the spectrum. Most of my students don't read because they are not very good at it.

Amy: How he contributed to people's understanding about young people with cancer in a very sensitive manner.

What would you say to a young person who's never read John Green's books?

Bottom line, there's one thing that young adult novels rarely are, and that's boring. They're built to grab your attention and hold it. And I'm not as young as I once was. At my age, I don't have time to be bored.
—Lev Grossman[21]

Madison: Read them now!

Skylar: Read them now!

Kim: Read them now! Even if you're not an avid reader, it's worth reading because it can open you up to more experiences and it will give you good knowledge about other kinds of people and different groups.

Liz: Get them. Read them. I will have them in my classroom and will recommend them to kids at every opportunity.

Bobby: I use his books all the time with my reluctant readers, many of whom are NOT readers. I'll give them a summary up until page 50 and tell them to jump in at page 50 and go from there. See where the book takes you. I've learned that a small group of guys who know that I'm reading the book (I reread the books with my students) with them will come in at lunch to discuss it with me. I've had really good luck with *Looking for Alaska* and *The Fault in Our Stars*. His books are gender neutral. The movie tends to make *The Fault in Our Stars* a "girl" book, but it's not.

Amy: I would strongly recommend *The Fault in Our Stars* (which I have done with some young people). This interview makes me want to read all of his books!

THE TAKEAWAY

I was at a school in Los Angeles last week, and a kid in a hoodie waited until everyone else had left before approaching me. "I read your book 'We Were Here' like three times," he said. His eyes were glassy and he kept fidgeting with his backpack straps. "Yo, that's my life in that book," he said. Then he took off.

—Matt de la Peña[22]

Skylar: I think some of the books you read in school most of the time are good books, but I feel like [if] we expose young adults to *different* kinds of literature, especially modern works, they'd be more encouraged to read. Whereas encouraging them to read older books that they have no interest in [makes them] think all books are like that. . . . There's a lot of themes of being your own person in [his] books, not worrying about necessarily what other people think about you . . . you don't have to be popular to have fun or to be [who] other people tell you to be.

Kim: You don't have to be a popular person to fit into a group of people. All these books were about people who didn't fit in. . . . You don't need to be part of the popular crew to have friends and have a good time. That's what I got out of it.

Jenn: I think about how I was a reader and how I wanted to find the books that would make me the reader my mom and my brother were; Green has written those books. This will be the book that will turn those students onto reading, and I can't wait to share that with my students.

Bobby: I have not and probably will not see *The Fault in Our Stars* movie. I liked the book, and it was just emotional enough for me to latch onto. It's reader response: I'm not looking at it from the main character's point of view but the parent's point of view. I didn't connect with Hazel's loss as much as a parent's loss. In the book, when Hazel's mother was always waiting for her, my father used to do that. And I do that with my kids. He'd always have a book in the car or something, and he'd wait for me. As a parent you get really good at waiting. Unfortunately, Hazel's parents were waiting for a tragic end, and that really spoke to me. I'm a father. I saw the different angles in the book, and to churn up those things on the big screen, I don't feel I need to go there.

READERS JUST WANT GOOD LITERATURE

On June 5, 2014, *Slate* writer Ruth Graham shook up the young adult world when she verbally shamed adults for "camping out" in bookstore shelves not intended for them. She further chastised the young adult genre, stating it "present[s] the teenage perspective in a fundamentally uncritical way." YA readers, according to Graham, are "asked to abandon mature insights," and therefore the literature is not intended for, nor should it be read by, adults. Using Green's book *The Fault in Our Stars* as a basis for her argument, she advocates for adult readers to explore the genre of books written with them in mind. After all, "life is short, and the list of great books for adults is so long." Graham identifies Hazel's problems—cancer aside—as simply "maudlin teen drama" masquerading a character that adults couldn't possibly relate to. In essence, adults crave—or should, according to Graham—more complex literature, the kind of works that only become "richer" as one grows older.[23] The interviews in this chapter, while only a minuscule sampling of Green's readership, were intended to solidify—no, celebrate—the notion that his books are written for selective, discriminating readers. Of course, a fifteen-year-old, young adult reader cannot connect with a book on the same intellectual level as a seventy-year-old licensed clinical psychologist. But the reading experience *can* be shared without stigmatizing the genre. John Green's novels transcend the notion that they are only written for adolescent readers; they cross over the boundaries traditionally set forth by literary snobs like Graham. Crossover novels connect generations of readers to the power of story. They fulfill the contractual obligation between the author and the reader. More important, they invite readers to get lost in a world *not* unlike their own.

NOTES

1. "New Study: 55% of YA Books Bought by Adults," *Publishers Weekly*, September 13, 2012.
2. Jonathan Stevens, "A Book by Any Other Name: Defining the Genre," *ALAN Review* 35, no. 1 (2007): 40–41.
3. Jonathan Hunt, "Redefining the Young Adult Novel," *Horn Book Magazine*, March/April 2007.
4. Maggie Stiefvater, "In Which Maggie Debates the Meaning of Crossover Fiction," *Maggie Stiefvater: The Official Blog*, June 28, 2012, accessed January 15, 2015, http://maggiestiefvater.com/.

5. Quoted in Colleen Mondor, "John Green and the Power of YA Books," Chasing Ray, October 2, 2006, accessed September 8, 2014, http://www.chasingray.com/.
6. Virginia R. Monseau, *Responding to Young Adult Literature* (Portsmouth, NH: Heinemann, 1999), 88.
7. Madison, interview by author Laura Brown, March 21, 2014.
8. Skylar, interview by author Laura Brown, March 21, 2014.
9. Kim, interview by author Laura Brown, March 21, 2014.
10. Liz, interview by author Kathy Deakin, July 23, 2014.
11. Jenn, interview by author Kathy Deakin, July 23, 2014.
12. Bobby, interview by author Kathy Deakin, July 23, 2014.
13. Amy, interview by author Kathy Deakin, July 23, 2014.
14. Monseau, *Responding to Young Adult Literature*, 97.
15. Ibid., xiii.
16. Matt de la Peña, "Seeing Themselves in Books," Room for Debate, *New York Times*, December 19, 2012.
17. Beth Yoke, "Why Expect More from Teenagers than Adults?" Room for Debate, *New York Times*, March 28, 2012.
18. Patricia McCormick, "When Authors Take Risks, That's Not Kids Stuff," Room for Debate, *New York Times*, March 28, 2012.
19. Chris Crutcher, "Young Adult Fiction: Let Teens Choose," *Huffington Post*, July 21, 2011.
20. de la Peña, "Seeing Themselves in Books."
21. Lev Grossman, "Nothing's Wrong with Strong Plot and Characters," Room for Debate, *New York Times*, March 28, 2012.
22. de la Peña, "Seeing Themselves in Books."
23. Ruth Graham, "Against YA: Read Whatever You Want; But You Should Feel Embarrassed When What You're Reading Was Written for Children," *Slate* Book Review, June 5, 2014.

Awards

BOOK AWARDS

Looking for Alaska: 2006 Michael L. Printz Award

The Michael L. Printz Award for Excellence in Young Adult Literature is an honor bestowed by a committee of nine. The award's namesake was a former school librarian with a passion for authors that write books for young adults. Fiction, nonfiction, poetry, and anthologies are selected based upon their literary merit; they represent the best writing in young adult literature.

An Abundance of Katherines: 2007 Michael L. Printz Award

Paper Towns: 2009 Edgar Allen Poe Award for Best Young Adult Mystery

The Edgar Allen Poe awards recognize works of fiction that highlight aspects of mystery and crime.

2010 Corine Literature Prize, Young Adult category

The Corine Literature Prize is a German literature prize that bestows awards on works of literary merit and public recognition.

***The Fault in Our Stars*: 2013 Children's Choice Book Award**

The Children's Choice Book Award is chosen by children and teen readers.

PERSONAL AWARDS

- 2012 Indiana Authors Award
- 2013 *Los Angeles Times* Book Prize
- 2014 MTVU Fandom Awards

Bibliography

Blasingame, James. *Books that Don't Bore 'Em: Young Adult Books that Speak to This Generation.* New York: Scholastic, 2007.

Cart, Michael. "Bold Books for Innovative Teaching: A Place of Energy, Activity, and Art." *English Journal* 93, no. 1 (2003): 113–15.

Crain, W. C. *Theories of Development.* New York: Prentice Hall, 1985.

Crutcher, Chris. "Young Adult Fiction: Let Teens Choose." *Huffington Post,* July 21, 2011.

de la Peña, Matt. "Seeing Themselves in Books." Room for Debate, *New York Times,* December 19, 2012.

Erikson, Erik. *Childhood and Society.* New York: Norton, 1963.

———. *Identity: Youth and Crisis.* New York: Norton, 1968.

Goodfriend, Wind. "A Psychologist at the Movies: Relationship Violence in 'Twilight.'" *Psychology Today,* November 9, 2011.

Graham, Ruth. "Against YA: Read Whatever You Want; But You Should Feel Embarrassed When What You're Reading Was Written for Children." *Slate* Book Review, June 5, 2014.

Green, John. *An Abundance of Katherines.* New York: Dutton, 2006.

———. *The Fault in Our Stars.* New York: Penguin, 2012.

———. *Looking for Alaska.* New York: Speak, 2005.

———. *Paper Towns.* New York: Dutton, 2008.

———. *Will Grayson, Will Grayson.* New York: Dutton, 2010.

Grossman, Lev. "Nothing's Wrong with Strong Plot and Characters." Room for Debate, *New York Times,* March 28, 2012.

Hamilton, Martha, and Mitch Weiss. *Children Tell Stories: Teaching and Using Storytelling in the Classroom.* 2nd ed. Katonah, NY: Richard C. Owen Publishers, 2005.

Hunt, Jonathan. "Redefining the Young Adult Novel." *Horn Book Magazine,* March/April 2007.

Johnson, Denise. "Teaching with Authors' Blogs: Connections, Collaboration, Creativity." *Journal of Adolescent and Adult Literacy* 54, no. 3 (February 2010): 172–80.

Kohlberg, Lawrence. *Essays on Moral Development.* Vol. 1: *The Philosophy of Moral Development.* San Francisco: Harper & Row, 1981.

McCormick, Patricia. "When Authors Take Risks, That's Not Kids Stuff." Room for Debate, *New York Times*, March 28, 2012.

Monseau, Virginia R. *Responding to Young Adult Literature*. Portsmouth, NH: Heinemann, 1999.

Publishers Weekly. "New Study: 55% of YA Books Bought by Adults." September 13, 2012.

Roxburgh, Stephen. "The Art of the Young Adult Novel." *ALAN Review* 32, no. 2 (2005): 4–10.

Stevens, Jonathan. "A Book by Any Other Name: Defining the Genre." *ALAN Review* 35, no. 1 (2007): 34–42.

Vine, Harold A., Jr., and Mark A. Faust. *Situating Readers: Students Making Meaning of Literature*. Urbana, IL: National Council of Teachers of English, 1993.

Whitney, Anne Elrod, Michael Ridgeman, and Gary Masquelier. "Beyond 'Is This Okay?' High School Writers Building Understandings of Genre." *Journal of Adolescent and Adult Literacy* 54, no. 7 (April 2011): 525–33.

Winchester, Laura E. "Depew School Board Committee Will Review 'Coming-of-Age' Novel." *Buffalo News*, February 7, 2008.

Wolk, Steven. "What Should Students Read?" *Phi Delta Kappan* 91, no. 7 (2010): 8–16.

Yoke, Beth. "Why Expect More from Teenagers than Adults?" Room for Debate, *New York Times*, March 28, 2012.

Index

125

About the Authors

Kathleen Deakin is an assistant professor at Metropolitan State University of Denver (MSU Denver) where she teaches classes in English education. A former high school English teacher in Gilbert, Arizona, Kathy enjoys helping teachers introduce young adult literature into their language arts classroom. After receiving her doctorate at Arizona State University in 2010, she moved to beautiful northern Colorado where she lives with her husband and her two teenagers.

Laura A. Brown is an assistant professor at the State University of New York in Potsdam, where she is the program coordinator for adolescent English education. Laura is a member of the Assembly on Literature for Adolescents of the National Council of Teachers of English and has presented at the ALAN Workshop and council's annual convention many times. Her work has appeared in the *ALAN Review* and the *Journal of Adolescent and Adult Literacy*. She is a former high school English teacher and writing specialist from Mesa, Arizona, where she was codirector of the Mesa Writing Project. She currently facilitates a writing/storytelling project between her students and residents of a local nursing home.

James Blasingame Jr. is an associate professor of English at Arizona State University (ASU) and director of the English education program. He is a past president of the Assembly on Literature for Adolescents of the National Council of Teachers of English and was the editor of the

ALAN Review, a professional journal devoted to young adult literature, from 2003 to 2009. He is the editor of the Print-Based Texts pages of the International Reading Association's *Journal of Adolescent and Adult Literacy* and winner of the International Reading Association's Arbuthnot Award for the 2008 outstanding university professor of young adult literature. He was named the ASU Parents Association Professor of the Year in 2008 and ASU Outstanding Doctoral Mentor in 2013. He has published over one hundred interviews with authors of adolescent literature and over three hundred book reviews. "Dr. B" was a high school English teacher, coach, and administrator for twenty-one years, in Iowa, Nebraska, Utah, and Kansas before completing his doctorate at the University of Kansas in 2000. He is a native of Cedar Rapids, Iowa.

CPSIA information can be obtained at www.ICGtesting.com
Printed in the USA
BVOW05*2135030615

402486BV00001BB/1/P

9 781442 249967